CAMBRIDGE LIBRARY COLLECTION

Books of enduring scholarly value

Printing and Publishing History

The interface between authors and their readers is a fascinating subject in its own right, revealing a great deal about social attitudes, technological progress, aesthetic values, fashionable interests, political positions, economic constraints, and individual personalities. This part of the Cambridge Library Collection reissues classic studies in the area of printing and publishing history that shed light on developments in typography and book design, printing and binding, the rise and fall of publishing houses and periodicals, and the roles of authors and illustrators. It documents the ebb and flow of the book trade supplying a wide range of customers with products from almanacs to novels, bibles to erotica, and poetry to statistics.

Progress in Printing and the Graphic Arts During the Victorian Era

First published in 1897, this is one of many books written by the technical journalist John Southward (1840–1902), one of the most prolific writers on printing in the nineteenth century. As the title indicates, Southward is primarily concerned with the development and progress of printing. Here he takes a thoroughly practical approach, surveying the different methods of printing and considering the improvements made in printing advertisements, books and newspapers, as well as to the different stages of the printing process itself. Southward's prose is clear and precise, and his style changes seamlessly from a narrative account of printing history to more instructional descriptions of printing methods. The book contains numerous illustrations and diagrams, and the pages are all lavishly decorated. This is a beautiful book, a thoroughly comprehensive account of the history and processes of printing from one of the leading nineteenth-century authorities on the subject.

Cambridge University Press has long been a pioneer in the reissuing of out-of-print titles from its own backlist, producing digital reprints of books that are still sought after by scholars and students but could not be reprinted economically using traditional technology. The Cambridge Library Collection extends this activity to a wider range of books which are still of importance to researchers and professionals, either for the source material they contain, or as landmarks in the history of their academic discipline.

Drawing from the world-renowned collections in the Cambridge University Library, and guided by the advice of experts in each subject area, Cambridge University Press is using state-of-the-art scanning machines in its own Printing House to capture the content of each book selected for inclusion. The files are processed to give a consistently clear, crisp image, and the books finished to the high quality standard for which the Press is recognised around the world. The latest print-on-demand technology ensures that the books will remain available indefinitely, and that orders for single or multiple copies can quickly be supplied.

The Cambridge Library Collection will bring back to life books of enduring scholarly value (including out-of-copyright works originally issued by other publishers) across a wide range of disciplines in the humanities and social sciences and in science and technology.

Progress in Printing and the Graphic Arts During the Victorian Era

JOHN SOUTHWARD

CAMBRIDGE
UNIVERSITY PRESS

CAMBRIDGE UNIVERSITY PRESS

Cambridge, New York, Melbourne, Madrid, Cape Town, Singapore,
São Paolo, Delhi, Dubai, Tokyo

Published in the United States of America by Cambridge University Press, New York

www.cambridge.org
Information on this title: www.cambridge.org/9781108009133

© in this compilation Cambridge University Press 2009

This edition first published 1897
This digitally printed version 2009

ISBN 978-1-108-00913-3 Paperback

Sir G. Hayter, R.A.

Her Majesty Queen Victoria in Coronation Robes.

Progress in Printing and the Graphic Arts during the Victorian Era.

BY

JOHN SOUTHWARD,

Author of "Practical Printing"; "Modern Printing"; "The Principles and Progress of Printing Machinery"; the Treatise on "Modern Typography" in the "Encyclopædia Britannica" *(9th Edition)*; "Printing" and "Types" in "Chambers's Encyclopædia" *(New Edition)*; "Printing" in "Cassell's Storehouse of General Information"; "Lessons on Printing" in Cassell's New Technical Educator," &c. &c.

LONDON:
SIMPKIN, MARSHALL, HAMILTON, KENT & CO. LTD.
1897.

The whole of the Roman Type in this Book has been set up by the Linotype Composing Machine, and machined direct from the Linotype Bars by Geo. W. Jones, Saint Bride House, Dean Street, Fetter Lane, London, E.C.   ❦ ❦ ❦ ❦ ❦ ❦ ❦

❧❧ Contents. ❧❧

CHAPTER I.

THIS cursory retrospect would have to be attempted in the spirit of the writer of the immortal treatise, "On Snakes in Ireland," if a dictum of the late Mr. William Morris could be accepted. That master of many arts declared that "no good printing had been done since 1550." Printing was at its zenith at the close of the first century of its existence. After then, no good printing, he said, was to be found.

I venture to protest against this view; and in the following pages hope to show that printing is by no means in a state of decadence. On the contrary, I will try to point out that very good printing is done. My contention is, in fact, that better printing has been done during the last sixty years—in each of the three principal branches of the business: job, news, and book printing—than was ever done before. To establish this it will only be necessary, I think, to contrast the workmanship, the appliances, the materials, of 1897 with those of 1837.

I begin with jobbing work, which might be regarded as the least important of the three branches of the printing business. Its products are more ephemeral than any others. A newspaper is often only read for half-an-hour, and is then thrown aside and forgotten. But the great bulk of jobbing work has a shorter life even than this. Much of it is instantly consigned to the waste-paper basket or the dust-heap. There is another peculiarity about it. It is not paid for by the person who is to become its possessor. We have to buy every other kind of printing, but this is given away. We do not pay for the circulars thrust into our letter-boxes, or the invoices sent us by our tradesmen. Hence it might be thought that any kind of work and material would do for jobbing. As a matter of fact, there is quite as much typographical skill expended on it as on bookwork.

MR. HORACE PORTER

IS at present personally engaged at Western Hall on large and important Photographic work, extending to the end of July, and while there he would be able to make any Photographs you may require, without charging for distance or travelling expenses.

SPECIMENS OF WORK AND ESTIMATES SUPPLIED.

Specialities: At Home Portraiture, Groups, Animals, Interiors and Exteriors.

Messrs. Pardonable & Pride, Western Street, W., say: "Your beautiful work is perfection itself."

HORACE PORTER,

SPECIALIST IN PHOTOGRAPHY,

864 BATTLE HILL, S.W.

JOBBING PRINTING OF THE PAST.

Again, its importance is shown by the preponderating number of persons constantly engaged in it—far more than in news and book-printing put together. Bookwork, as a special branch, is done in only two dozen towns throughout the kingdom; there is hardly a respectably-sized village without its jobbing printer. There are, perhaps, only about 2,000 news-paper printing establishments (for some of them do several different papers); there are at least 8,000 general jobbing offices.

The character of jobbing printing depends to a large extent upon the ornamental types used in it. Now, at the beginning of the present century there were no ornamental types of any kind; if display was required it had to be obtained by some novel disposition of plain romans, italics, or blacks. Not long before the Queen came to the throne, however, there arose a demand for something more ornate and decorative. The founders

responded to this demand by providing type styles which were copied mainly from the lettering of the writing masters, imitating their absurd and inelegant flourishes and pen-shading; from that of the painters who "wrote" shop facias; and that of copper-plate engravers, who often in engraving cards and book-plates combined the eccentricities of the painters with the affectations of the writing masters. The result was a style of type faces which was simply execrable. Examples of them are given in

THE SCOTS LODGE

OF THE

Most Ancient and Honourable Fraternity of Free and
Accepted Masons, No. 2319, England.

W. BRO. JOSEPH J. WHITEHEAD,

Worshipful Master.

BURNS

ANNIVERSARY

BANQUET,

ON

Thursday, the 23rd January, 1896,

AT

THE SCOTS CORPORATION HALL,

CRANE COURT, FLEET STREET,

LONDON.

JOBBING PRINTING OF THE PAST.

Burns ❧ Anniversary Banquet. ❦

The : Scots : Lodge of the ✴✴✴✴✴✴✴✴✴✴✴✴ Most Ancient and ❦❦❦ Honourable Fraternity of Free and ♣♣♣♣♣♣♣♣♣ ♣♣♣♣♣ Accepted Masons, ❦❦❦ No. 2319, England, W. Bro. ♣♣♣♣♣♣♣♣♣ ♣♣ Joseph J. Whitehead, ❦❦❦ Worshipful Master.

The Scots Corporation Hall, Crane : Court : Fleet : St. London : on : Thursday, the : 23rd : January, ✴✴✴ 1896 ✴✴✴

JOBBING WORK—STYLE OF THE PRESENT DAY.

9

these pages. These letters expose an utter want of taste on the part of their designers. This had its parallel in a want of taste on the part of those who used the types. They thought that all sorts of jobs should be set up in "monumental" style, which was a combination of the style of lettering on a modern title page and on a tombstone. Its leading feature is that lines should be alternated in regard to length—a big line was to be followed by a little one; and then a big one should come in, and so on. Further, each of these lines should occupy the middle of the measure of the composition; if it was short, half the space must go before the line and half after it. The specimens presented exhibit the system as then followed. The long lines were said to be "full out," and the little ones were the catch-lines. The supposed necessity for certain lines to be "full out" led to the fashioning of some of the most awkward letters imaginable. The principal line might consist of only one word, which if set in a letter of normal proportions would be too short. Hence outrageously "extended" letters were produced. If these were not sufficient to fill up the measure, spaces were put between them. To meet cases where the wording would not otherwise come into the line, extremely attenuated or "condensed" letters were cut. These very wide and very narrow letters were unsightly and unreadable. It was another canon of bad taste never to set a leading line in lower-case, although lower-case letters are nearly always more legible a little distance off than capitals.

These rules prevailed up to within the last twenty years, and no printer dared to contravene them. An altogether different style now prevails, and its existence marks a progress of the most decided and valuable character. The new style is characterised by freedom from conventional restraints; a commonsense and logical grouping of words; and the introduction, within due bounds, of appropriate ornamentation. It is recognised by the printers that excellence consists in making the composition attractive, and the object of its production—whether a card or a circular—apparent at a glance, in giving full prominence to prominent expressions; in refraining from making big lines merely because he possesses big type, and little ones because he has narrow type. He sees that there is really no reason, in the nature of things, why wording should be divided into centred lines like those of the tombstone. Instead of covering all the available space with lines needlessly long or needlessly large, he either leaves blanks, which contrast with the lettering and emphasise it, or fills up the vacant spaces with appropriate ornaments, which add to utility—beauty. Much more discrimination is now shown than at any previous period in the selection of type. The extravagantly ornate types are quite in disfavour. Purer and simpler styles are sought for ; and more attention is paid to originality of treatment, symmetry and harmony, and general effectiveness.

Another decided mark of progress is shown in the greater use of colours than formerly, and of different kinds of colours. At the beginning of the reign the average printer possessed only two colours—red and blue. These were, as a rule, raw and gaudy. He obtained his chromatic effects—such as they were—by ringing the changes on these, with an admixture of black lines. Some printers had green and yellow, and these formed the limit of the typographical colour-box. The few colours were used with extravagance or with niggardliness, according to the price to be received for the job, and with little regard to appropriateness or harmony. For some years these primary colours have been nearly abandoned, except for admixture with others forming new and more subdued tints and art shades. Besides inks, dry colours are supplied which can be made into inks by the admixture with them of varnishes. There will be used such tints as rose, salmon, blue, citron-yellow, sea-green, buff, mauve, grey ; in shades green-black, blue-black, and brown. The colour scheme for a circular may include chromotype-yellow, chromotype-red with equal part varnish, milori-blue and varnish, burnt umber, chocolate-brown, olive-green, black—all varieties of hues unattempted by the printer sixty years ago. He had not the colours ; if he had possessed them he would not have had the taste or the skill to use them. Advances in art education largely account for this progress. The public have plainly shown a disposition to remunerate printers for doing more artistic work. The demand for it created the supply, and when printers called for the means of doing such work, the ink-makers bestirred themselves to provide what was wanted. We have not yet attained to the excellence in colour printing of some of our foreign rivals, but during the last few years we have undoubtedly made great advances.

Great progress in jobbing work has been brought about by the introduction of the small platen machine. Nearly all work up to quarto is now done on one of these convenient presses ; some of them, of course, print far larger formes. Their general use dates back less than thirty years, for they were brought into this country only in 1866, although Gordon, the American engineer, invented his " Franklin Press," of which the English machine was a copy, in 1858. Printers were slow in appreciating their merits, but as soon as they were understood, it was seen that they were going to effect important changes in the business. Previously, work of this kind was done at a press, on which, with a boy rolling and a man pulling, 250 commercial cards could be printed in an hour. A quick platen machine will now do 2,000. The public used to be charged for 500 of such cards about 7s. 6d., but 1,000 of them are now done for 4s. 6d. Handbills, which in the old press days were about 5s. per 1,000, are now charged 8s. 6d. for 10,000, and so on. This has been brought about by the use of the small platen, which can be worked by one boy. But the printing is not only done more rapidly and more cheaply, but ever so much better. A foolscap folio machine is enormously stronger than a foolscap folio press of any kind. The latter gives a spongy, yielding impression, owing to the blanket between the tympans; the other gives a hard, unyielding impression, clear and bright. The public would not now tolerate the business cards, for instance, that were accepted sixty years ago. There must not be the slightest impression on the back, and with a press blanket this is unavoidable, to some extent, at least; while it is wholly unnecessary when a machine with hard packing is used.

The comparative inexpensiveness of platen-machine printing has had much to do with the extended practice of colour-printing. One thousand copies of a circular to be printed in four colours on a press would occupy two men, or a man and a boy, about a day. The work could be done by a boy alone in half a day at machine. Besides the better impression of the latter, there is much better register, which is of great importance in colour work.

Turning to a different kind of jobbing work, a word may be said about posters, or placards, or bills, as they are indifferently called. The difference between those of 1897 and 1837 would astonish the younger generation. Sixty years ago such work was always done at a press, and the largest sheet that was printed was a double demy, 22 by 25 inches, an area of about 550 square inches. Poster machines are now made which print a sheet 74 by 45 inches—an area of 3,330 inches. The quad-double crown machine is quite common; it prints 2,400 square inches. About 150 per hour, with two men working, alternately rolling and pulling, was the speed of a press. The last-named machine can be run at about 500 to 600 per hour, and the large sheet can, by the addition of rotary cutters to the machine, be divided into 4, making 2,000 to 2,400 sheets per hour, against the 150 of the press. Flyers are fitted, so that less labour is called for.

The improved appearance of a quad-double demy sheet as compared with that of four-double demy sheets—however carefully the bill-poster may piece them—need not be referred to. Many large-sized modern placards are printed from one block. No press whatever could print them; no press would be big or strong enough. Hence the posters that embellish—

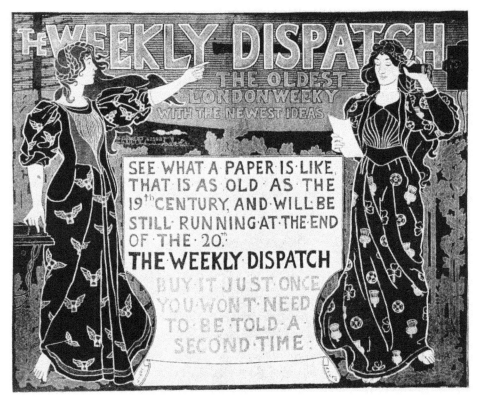

MODERN ART POSTER. DESIGNED BY LOUIS RHEAD.

or, at least, except in the opinion of the most æsthetic individuals, do not disfigure our walls—are entirely the creation of the last few years. They were not possible before engineers built the large machines now procurable.

Quite recently, a new kind of placard, known as the "art poster," has appeared upon our walls. The style came from abroad. A small library of books detailing the history of this modern fashion has appeared, but there is no room here to go into its origin. The art poster differs from ordinary picture posters by its stiffness of design and its huge masses of brilliant colour. Few colours are used—perhaps four or six. These are not overlapped as in ordinary colour printing, but are, as it is called, silhouetted. Each is untouched by the other, like the colours in a coloured map. There is quite a craze just now for such things. Advertisers pay large prices for designs of this kind, and a few artists who possess the peculiar ability to make such designs are prospering upon it. Other kinds of placards also of the art kind adorn our walls. Some are in black and white only, and some have the effect of a fine oil or water-colour painting. The best artists, members of the Royal Academy, and other distinguished people, are now not averse to design these posters if the fee is attractive. Printers are easily found who are able to render every effect intended by the designer. Improvements in printing machines and ink render this possible. Anyone who walks about the streets and is not blind has ocular demonstration of vast progress in this particular direction.

A word may here be said as to recent progress in the printing of illustrated catalogues for manufacturers, and to similar publications. The perfection to which this branch of the business has been brought within the last few years is remarkable. It is largely owing to American competition. Over there business firms were prepared to pay extremely high prices for very superior work. To undertake such work, a printer had to possess the finest presses and the most modern types. He had to use the most costly paper and the best inks. Up to a short time ago we had not in this country any of these requisites—the presses, the type, the paper, the ink. There was no call on the part of English firms for such luxurious printing, and no English printer attempted it. If he had done so he would have had to import the machinery and materials. At last our manufacturers began to realise that it was necessary to distribute as good catalogues as their American and other rivals. Printers were found who attempted the work. Their number has since grown considerably, and is now growing, and some of their printing is quite equal to the average of that done abroad. Exquisite specimens, excelling the best book work, are often thus got out, and no one who wishes to form any idea of the progress of our art can ignore these things, although they are generally printed for free distribution. Unfortunately, there are few English-made machines which are capable of printing them. The best catalogues are, for the present, nearly all done on one of the American-built machines.

CHAPTER II.

PROGRESS IN NEWSPAPER PRINTING—DIFFICULTIES ARISING FROM THE
NECESSITIES OF RAPID PRINTING—THE REAM AND THE REEL.

HE slightest comparison of the newspapers which describe
the Jubilee celebrations and those which recorded the
Accession will show that the former are very much better
printed than the latter were. This fact is of increased
interest when we regard the difficulties in printing to which
modern developments have given rise. A newspaper of any considerable
circulation at the present day is not printed by a flat-bed machine, and
on sheets of paper, each carefully damped before being fed into the machine. There are a few machines of the rotary kind which print from
movable type, in order to save the expense of stereotyping, but they are
quite exceptional. Practically, printing of this kind is done from stereotype
plates cast either from movable type or linotype bars.

When the Linotype system was introduced five or six years ago many newspaper managers of experience thought that it would result in a deterioration
of the quality of newspaper printing. They could understand the economy
it promised to effect in composition, but they could not realise that a cast
from what appeared to be a mere stereotype of a line would be equal to
one from an original type surface. They forgot that the bar was as much
an original surface as the type. Both are cast from matrices. Only one
casting is involved in the production of either. There is no real reason
why the composite cast, which we term the bar, and the single cast, which

is called the type, should not be exactly alike as regards all the qualities of good founding. One can be made as sharp and as accurate as the other. In depth of face, so important a consideration in making plates, the linotype may be better than the type. As a matter of fact, the linotyped newspapers are now better specimens of printing than the typed ones. And they are not only better specimens occasionally, but permanently. It is very easy to perceive that a paper has just been printed from new founts of type, for it presents a very remarkable comparison with the issue of the day previously, when the founts were old and worn by the heating and beating of the stereo process. The linotype newspaper is always the same.

The general improvement to be noticed in newspaper printing at the present day has been achieved in the face of other difficulties. Amongst them are the difficulties arising from the immense increase in the circulations of newspapers of late years. Enormous numbers of copies have to be printed within a limited time, on machines speeded up to 10,000 or 12,000 impressions per hour per reel—or about 200 per minute. The plates have to be cast in an astonishingly short space of time. Our newspapers are now so large that very cheap paper has to be used. One penny is the general price for a morning paper and a halfpenny for an evening paper. A morning journal, as elsewhere mentioned, may consist of from eight to sixteen pages. It would be ruinous to use the paper of sixty years ago— even if sufficient of it could be produced. Cheap paper, made of cheap materials, is alone commercially possible, and it is necessarily much inferior in regard to substance and strength than that formerly used. It has to be printed from reels, instead of reams, at a speed corresponding to that of a train covering thirty or forty miles an hour. Owing to the class of paper used, an ink specially adapted to the conditions of rotary printing at high speed on thin weak paper has to be used. It is greatly to the credit of the engineer that these difficulties have been overcome, and that a morning newspaper of 1897 done on a rotary machine is so much better a specimen of typography than the newspaper of 1837 produced from type on a flat-surfaced slow printing machine.

Our newspapers are now much larger than formerly, as elsewhere pointed out, and they may soon be larger still. The invention of supplement in-setting machines has rendered easy the enlargement of a paper whenever necessary. To-day, a sixteen-page paper, of seven long columns each, is not remarkable. It consists of 112 columns, and as the

Caxton Window, St. Margaret's, Westminster.

papers of 1837 were mostly "folios of four pages," each containing six columns, one journal now represents eight journals then.

Much of the type used is smaller than formerly, and several new sizes have been introduced, chiefly for advertisements, with a view to getting as many lines as possible in a column. The faces of new founts have somewhat altered, with the view of doing away with the kerns, which are so liable to break off in beating the stereo flong. During the last few years the tendency has been towards greater legibility of face, broader and heavier founts being preferred to the light and condensed ones formerly in vogue. This change is in itself an improvement. Italics are being disused, to a great extent, for proper names, such as those of journals, ships, etc.—a change which is also to be commended. Long articles, such as speeches, are broken up into paragraphs with cross-headings. Following the American style, bold jobbing or titling founts are used for the headings of articles of news, although we do not yet occupy one-third of a column with headings to an item of the same or of less length. Fancy types are more freely used in the advertisement pages, and blocks are more often permitted. Not many years ago, many a first-class daily paper would accept at no price an advertisement set up in jobbing types and including a block. Nowadays, an advertiser can usually get his matter set up in the office of his advertising agent in any style he pleases, and it will be admitted, if he pays for it. Illustrations are far more numerous than ever, and, although they are printed on fast rotaries, are infinitely superior to the illustrations occasionally given in the early years of the reign. This is particularly conspicuous in the beautiful and most artistic illustrations which from time to time appear in the "Daily Chronicle." They are sharp and bright, bear plenty of colour, and are printed without the slightest slur. They show what can be done with process blocks even on the fastest web machine. But not only as regards illustrations, but in general typography, it may be claimed that our newspapers are the best in the world, and they have become so by the steady progress of the last half century in the mechanics of the art of printing.

CHAPTER III.❧❧❧

PROGRESS IN BOOK PRINTING—USE OF TYPOGRAPHICAL ORNAMENTS—
IMPROVED METHODS AND APPLIANCES—PROCESS ILLUSTRATIONS.

T the commencement of the present century, the " Biblio-
mania" was raging in this country. One of its outcomes
was the issue of a series of sumptuous books, printed by
Bensley, Bulmer, and other famous contemporary printers.
Some of the books were produced regardless of expense,
being intended for a few wealthy collectors who were prepared to pay
lavishly for them. Amongst such books may be mentioned the magnificent
volumes of Dr. T. Frognall Dibdin, especially his " Bibliographical Decameron."
It exemplifies the very highest attainable standard prevailing at the time.
Comparing them with the work executed in the best book houses of the
present day, it must be confessed that the printing was not up to what
would now be expected, especially in books published at such high prices.
The handsome appearance of Dibdin's and other books is derived from the
large margins, the wide spacing of the lines, the wood engravings, and
above all, the copper-plates. The wood-cuts are beautifully engraved, but
they are poorly printed. The copper-plates for present purposes may be
left out of consideration, as they are not printed by a letterpress method.
Anyone comparing the " Decameron" with a book of the present year, such
as Nansen's "Voyage of the Fram," must be impressed with the great advances made during the last half century.

The progress which has been made is, however, best shown by the
ordinary run of books, not by exceptional achievments in any one year

It began soon after 1828, when Charles Whittingham became associated with the publisher and bibliophile, William Pickering. These two men were continually in each other's society, ever planning some improvement in book-making. The late Henry Stevens describes them as "working for many years harmoniously together. It was their custom to each first sit upon every new book, and painfully hammer out in his own mind its ideal form and proportions. Then two Sundays at least were required to compare notes in the little summer-house in Mr. Whittingham's garden at Chiswick, or in the after-dinner sanctuary, to settle the shape and dress of their forthcoming 'friend of man.' It was amusing, as well as instructive, to see each of them when they met pull from his bulging side-pocket well-worn title pages and sample leaves for discussion and consideration. When they agreed, perfection was at hand, and the 'copy' went forward to the compositors, but not till then."

About 1840, Mr. Whittingham's office, the Chiswick Press, acquired an unrivalled collection of head and tail pieces, borders, and other typographical ornaments. No other printer in Europe could boast of a similar collection, either in regard to number or excellence. The best books of the great printers were searched for designs, and these, if approved of, were copied. Many of them afforded suggestions for better designs, and these suggestions were carried out. This enterprise, carried out almost without consideration of its costliness, together with the splendid printing done at the Chiswick Press, was the beginning of the forward movement in England and Scotland. Other printers were compelled to make an effort to rival Mr. Whittingham. Previously, their ordinary so-called ornaments were mean and distasteful to a degree. They were usually made up of what we would now call pieces of "border," but were then called "flowers," and were sold by the type-founders at so much a pound. Inartistic printers formed squares and rectangles of them, in the way in which mosaic flooring is made. Whittingham's example changed all this. The founders soon found it necessary to engage artists to design head and tail pieces, which were cut in wood, and sold in the form of casts to printers. Even cheap books at once gave evidence of improvement; and progress has gone on up to the present day.

In 1843, the era of "old-style" printing was ushered in, and for this again we are indebted to Whittingham. As mentioned elsewhere, he obtained in that year founts from the original matrices of the first William

Caslon. So well were he and his publisher, Pickering, satisfied with the result of the experiment, that other volumes were printed in the same style. Then followed, on the part of other printers, a demand for old forms of romans. In 1850, Messrs. Miller and Richard commenced cutting a beautiful series of founts of this character, and other founders brought out founts in rivalry. The public eye was soon educated to require a higher standard of bookwork, and it soon obtained it.

Much of the improvement which has since been effected is due to the paper-makers, the ink-makers, and especially the engineers. Some of the progress made in these appliances and materials will be referred to in subsequent chapters. Provided with better materials the printers could go forward. In 1837 books of small circulation were printed on hand presses, those of large circulation on Cowper and Applegath machines. The system of wetting the paper was universal, and combined with the use of soft blankets gave the rough impression previously mentioned in connection with jobbing work. The Cowper machines gave much coarser impressions than are the rule nowadays. Nor was their register as accurate as is now insisted on. A newspaper is now as well printed as a book was then. Gradually this plan was abandoned, and, as it has been stated in another chapter, the very highest class of bookwork is done on dry paper with the hardest impression possible; not, however, the heaviest.

This new style of printing was originated in America, for the purpose of printing fine wood-cuts. In 1838, Messrs. Harper, the New York publishers, determined to issue an illustrated Bible, which should be superior, from a typographical point of view, to anything previously achieved. The superintendence of the printing was entrusted to Joseph A. Adams, of the same city. He was originally a printer, but afterwards learned the art of wood-engraving, which he followed successfully. To him is due the honour of having originated fine wood-cut printing, by introducing the two features of building up the overlays for the cuts, and printing them by hard packing, on a powerful machine. This was, in the history of typography, an epoch-making book. It led to a whole series of changes, the influence of which were not confined to America. The greatest of all improvements has been brought about by the success of some American serials, containing fine illustrations. About 1870, Theo L. DeVinne, of New York, undertook the printing of some of these, and determined to surpass anything which had hitherto been accomplished. He carried still further the principle of hard packing, and of overlaying. He initiated, however, another change, which has been productive of the most important results. He printed on dry paper. This involved an improvement in ink, for what was adapted for damp paper was not adapted for dry. He abandoned the prevailing system of pressing the paper after printing it. The result was a magazine of a style previously undreamt of. For some years the American monthlies were, as specimens of fine magazine printing, superior to any in the world, and this superiority was due to the reforms brought about directly or indirectly by this great printer. It is only lately that we have attempted to emulate his work, but to do so we have had to resort to American and German presses. There are in existence several English magazines which do not suffer by comparison with any foreign ones; but it has taken many years to bring wood-cut printing to this perfection.

In this connection wood-cut printing must be taken as covering process blocks. These have now nearly supplanted wood-cut work. For a long time one leading illustrated newspaper refused to admit such blocks into its pages, and at first the refusal was justified. The blocks were hard and scratchy to a degree, and their lines were often broken. Typographic etchings, as they were then called, were used only because they were cheaper than wood-cuts. In time they were improved, and photography hastened the improvement. Artists of higher rank permitted their drawings to be thus reproduced, and wood-engraving entered upon the down grade. Eventually, the half-tone process was introduced from Germany. Its method did not long remain a secret, and several firms produced this kind of blocks. Most of them, it is to be noticed, are now located in the northern suburbs of London.

The leading illustrated journals now use process blocks, almost to the complete exclusion of wood-cuts. The popularity of the half-tone block is one of the facts of the present time. It has even brought into existence a new kind of literature, depending for its attractiveness upon the pictures. As a rule, the printing of these blocks is not as well done in England as in America. Printers account for this by the higher prices paid in America for printing. This is, to a certain extent, true, but probably the best explanation of our inferiority in this particular is the weakness and insufficient inking and distributing capacity of our presses, and the ineptitude of many of our pressmen. Already efforts are being made to remedy both of these shortcomings.

While acknowledging this, it is not fair to ignore the high standard of our general bookwork. It is not inferior to that of any other country in the world. This is more especially obvious in regard to cheap books, such as reprints of non-copyright books, issued for a few pence each. They are, as a rule, in all respects admirable specimens of typography. They are printed on thin, cheap paper, but it has generally received a fine, but not excessive, polish, by being rolled before printing. The printing is usually done without damping, and thus destroying the surface of the paper. The types make little or no indentation; both sides of the paper are usually smooth and glossy. The ink is black, and the colour full, but not smudgy. The type used has been fresh and clear, and the plate taken from it has been sharp and deep. It may have been printed direct from linotyped bars, or from stereos of linotype bars, and it may be impossible to distinguish the type from the linotype. The register is always accurate. Process blocks are freely introduced, and, as a rule, they are well, if not quite perfectly, made ready, and brought up. Sixty years ago there were cheap books, but they did not show these qualities. In every element of good workmanship, the book of to-day is as superior to that of 1837, as the locomotive of to-day is to that of the time of Robert Stephenson.

CHAPTER IV.

THE HAND PRESS—THE IMPROVED WOODEN PRESS—EARL STANHOPE AND HIS
PRESS—THE COLUMBIAN PRESS—THE ALBION PRESS—THEIR CAPABILI-
TIES—THE COMPOSITION ROLLER.

IN order to realise, even in an imperfect degree, the enormous progress which has been made in the art of printing
during the Victorian era, it is necessary to recall the construction and capabilities of the appliances which were in
use when, in 1837, Her Majesty ascended the throne.
Nearly all printing from type and from wood engravings was then done on
the hand press, of which there were then three principal styles in use.

The oldest of these was the wooden press, which was in principle probably
identical with that used by Gutenberg in 1450, although improvements had
been made in it, in the early part of the
seventeenth century, by a Dutch astro-
nomer and printer, Blaew. The press had
a stone bed; the platen of mahogany was
so small that only about half a sheet of
demy could be properly printed by one
pull of the bar; for a larger sheet the
carriage had to be run still further in, and
another impression given. The accompanying illustration, reduced from John-

WOODEN PRESS IN USE IN
1837.

son's "Typographia," gives an accurate view of what was known as the
"Improved Wooden Press," as arranged for bookwork, by having a frisket

attached, four pieces of which were cut out, to correspond with the number of pages in the forme to be printed.

The first really great improver of the hand printing press was Charles Mahon, third Earl Stanhope. Of this remarkable man no memoir was written until the present year, when Mr. Horace Hart, Controller of the Oxford University Press, compiled one for the "Collectanea" of the Oxford Historical Society. The fragmentary papers left by Earl Stanhope were placed at the disposal of the author by the present Earl, who also permitted the copying of the only portrait in existence of his noble ancestor—a painting by Thomas Gainsborough, which was never finished, owing to the death of the artist. It is reproduced here in miniature, by permission. The papers show that the Earl was (in the words of Mr. Horace Hart) a man of "untiring industry, of wide sympathies, of unstinted generosity, and greatly in advance of his time in many ways." In the "Memoirs of Sir N. W. Wraxall, he is thus described: "His ardent, zealous, and impetuous mind, tinged with deep shades of republicanism and eccentricity, which extended even to his dress and manners, was especially marked by a bold originality of character, very enlightened views of the public welfare or amelioration, inflexible pertinacity, and a steady uprightness of intention. His eccentricities of dress, character, and deportment, however great they might be, were nevertheless allied to extraordinary powers of elocution, as well as energies of mind. A man who at every period of his life, whether as a commoner or a peer, displayed the same ardent, eccentric, fearless, indefatigable, and independent character."

EARL STANHOPE.

Such was the man to whom we owe the first important improvement in printing presses that was effected in the course of three centuries and a half. His press—of which a view is here given—was entirely of iron. The platen was double the size of that of the wooden press. The straight bar and screw of the old wooden press was abandoned, and there was adopted instead a system of links and levers. The approach and withdrawal of the platen were thus rendered more rapid, and the fullest amount of pressure was obtained just at the right moment. The first press was finished in 1800, and its powers were tried in the office of a celebrated printer of that day—William Bulmer. Johnson, in his "Typographia" (1824), speaks of the "very extraordinary power of the Stanhope presses when contrasted with that of the wooden ones"; but adds an experience of his own concerning the printing of a wood-cut then considered to be of abnormal dimensions—namely, 15 by 11½ inches —or about the size of a full-page block in one of our present illustrated newspapers. "We attempted to pull a proof; the block was well beat over and ink twice taken, a damp piece of india paper was laid upon it and a blanket, with a second one inside the tympans, when the bar was well pulled down by two men for several seconds, with all the power that could be applied to the press; but to our utter astonishment we found little more than would have appeared from a plain block. At length, after considerable labour and the

STANHOPE PRESS IN USE IN 1837.

greatest risk of breaking the press, we obtained a few inferior impressions, by means of three blankets and other expedients. We have no hesitation in stating this to have been the greatest power ever applied to a Stanhope press."

This statement is interesting for several reasons. It shows how weak, compared with modern appliances, were the strongest presses of the period. It also indicates the limited dimensions of the wood engravings then printed. It further points out by what means alone any kind of an impression could be obtained—by the use of damp paper and a soft material in the tympan. This style of printing, as already mentioned, has since been entirely abandoned, in favour of dry paper and hard packing—but the use of these was rendered possible only by the construction of the powerful machines which in the course of this retrospect will be referred to when we have to describe the evolution of that mammoth press, the modern machine.

The next improver of the printing press was George Clymer, a mechanic, of Pennsylvania, who introduced to England, in 1817, the Columbian Press. Amongst his improvements were the greater efficiency and range of the bar, and the increased strength given to the essential parts of the press. The platen was attached to a powerful lever, by means of a square bar working in guides. The heavy eagle ornament

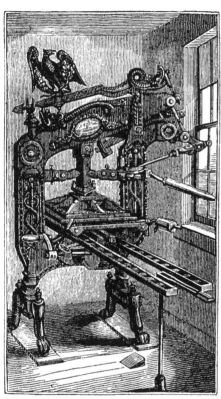

COLUMBIAN PRESS IN USE IN 1837.

shown on the head, in the block annexed, was a counterpoise to secure the self-acting recovery of the platen. In an address which Clymer issued to the printers of London in 1818 he says: "Much as my predecessors have done towards improving and perfecting that most important machine, the printing press, it is evident from the corroborating testimonies annexed, that if I have not yet brought it to the greatest possible perfection, I have approached much nearer than any who have preceded me." He claims that his press is superior alike on the ground of superabundant power and me- chanical precision of impression, and greater facility in working the largest formes. Johnson, in his "Typographia," already mentioned, gives an anecdote which may show to what extent this increased strength had been obtained. He states that he had two of these presses in use. He was, in fact, one of the best prac-

tical printers of his day. "We flatter ourselves that we have put the Columbian press to a much greater test, with respect to power, than any of the printers of Europe, or even the United States." This achievement consisted in printing the block, above referred to, of which even a satisfactory proof could not be got by the Stanhope press. He gives a graphic account of the operation of printing this "extensive and most curious engraving." It was composed of seven pieces of wood, through which were placed four strong iron bolts with nuts at each end to draw the wood close together. "We next found that even the Columbian press, of which so much has been said of its extraordinary power, was not sufficient for this block. Consequently we had a new bar made, considerably larger than usual, which was so bent that it just left sufficient room for the tympans to rise and fall, otherwise it went so far over that a man could not conveniently reach it. Even this had not the desired effect, so we next resolved upon having about two inches taken off the connecting rod, which enabled us to accomplish our object with regard to the impression ; but, notwithstanding we had thus increased the power, we found it necessary to have two stout men. Having now gained sufficient power, we were next at a loss for ink which would answer the purpose ; that of different ink makers were then tried, but each failed in some respect or other ; therefore we at length resorted to the expedient of mixing several of them together, which proved much better ; but still that would not do, and we were then compelled to have recourse to an addition of some other ingredients by which means it was at length accomplished." This reminiscence recalls not only the weakness

ALBION PRESS IN USE IN
1837.

of the press, but the imperfection of the materials to the hand of the pressman. How since those days the art of ink-making has been revolutionised will be noticed subsequently.

Clymer, on coming over to England, made an arrangement with a London engineer, R. W. Cope, to manufacture his presses for a period of ten years. In 1820, however, Cope brought out a press of his own, which he called the "Albion Press." This was never patented and possessed little novelty, for important parts of it were copied from the Stanhope and from a French press invented by Anisson-Duperron. Cope's press was so strong, so light, and so true in its work that it at once gained favour amongst printers, and it has not, up to the present day, been wholly superseded. The pull was very easy, and the press generally more convenient and quicker to work than the Columbian.

In the picture of the wooden press there will be seen affixed to the near side of the frame the shelf or box in which were contained the "balls" that were used for inking the type. They were made of cotton wool covered with skins or pelts, which had to be continuously "soaked" to keep them in proper order. This was done in an abominably filthy manner, and a printing office of that day was more offensive than a common sewer is now. Here is the process of inking a forme by "beating" with balls. "The pressman imagines, or by his eye judges, the length of his forme divided into four equal parts or rows. He places his left-hand ball at the hither end of the first row, so that though the ball be round, yet the square encompassed within that round shall sufficiently cover so much of the square of the hither end of that row as it is well capable to cover; and his right hand ball he sets upon the hither end of the third row; he sets his ball close upon the face of the letter with the handles of the ball stock a little bending towards him; but as he presses them upon the face of the letter, he mounts them perpendicular, and lifting at once both the balls lightly just clear off the face of the letter, he removes them about the fifth part of the breadth of the forme towards the further side of the forme, and again sets them close down upon the face of the letter. Thus beating from the hither towards the further side is, in pressman's phrase, called going up the forme. Having thus gone twice upwards and twice downwards with the balls, the forme is sufficiently beaten when the face of the letter takes well." The shelf shown in the engraving formed the "ink block." The ink was daubed inside this block and distributed by a "brayer"—a piece of wood turned to a round shape and flat on the bottom—and a "slice," a short iron shovel. When not in use, the balls were kept on the racks, or pegs, on the near cheek of the press, which are also represented in the engraving.

This part of presswork was very laborious, as well as extremely unpleasant. The men who performed it were of the roughest character. Office regulations or "chapel rules" provided penalties—called "solaces," somewhat ironically—for swearing, fighting, and being drunk in the chapel —offences which are practically unknown in present-day printing offices. Intemperance, indeed, was quite an ordinary characteristic of the pressmen. It was thought that unless he imbibed huge quantities of beer he could not discharge his duties. In the picture of the Stanhope press a foaming tankard of beer is one of the most prominent features. When Benjamin Franklin came to London to work as a printer he chose presswork conceiving that he had need of bodily exercise, to which he had been accustomed in America. The habit of drinking no stimulants whatever gained for him the nickname of "The Aquatic American." This incident was depicted in a painting by Mr. Eyre Crow, R.A., exhibited at the Royal Academy, in 1858, and which is here reproduced. Although the period represented is long anterior to that of Queen Victoria, the customs depicted were not abandoned at the time when Her Majesty came to the throne, when the potman with his pots of "fourpenny" was a constant visitor to the printing office. The picture also accurately represents the wooden

BENJAMIN FRANKLIN IN A LONDON PRINTING OFFICE.

press itself, being drawn from a press in the office where Franklin worked. The press is now in the South Kensington Museum.

Earl Stanhope made many experiments with the view of superseding the filthy old pelts. He tried skin, cylinders, silk, and other material, without success. In 1811, Donkin, the inventor of an impracticable printing machine, hit upon a mixture of glue and treacle, a composition which it is stated was then used in the Potteries for transferring designs printed upon paper on to earthenware. In 1818, Edward Cowper, whose name will be mentioned presently, invented the modern ink table and the composition roller—two of the most important inventions made in the history of printing. They are shown, somewhat indistinctly, in the background of the portrait which we present on a later page. Great opposition was at first raised to the innovation, especially on the part of the pressmen, although the appliance was calculated to alleviate so materially the hard conditions of their labour. Chiefly through the perseverance of Robert Harrild, the rollers were gradually introduced, and ultimately superseded the pelt balls. Without rollers of somewhat similar substance and qualities modern fast printing would have been impossible.

The treacle in this composition was used to make the hard glue soft and springy. The mixture was adopted exclusively for many years, although it had various disadvantages. A treacle roller, when kept in a dry place, became as hard as a brick within a month or six weeks, unless the moisture it was continually losing was replenished by daily washings with water. The continual evaporation and absorption was not only a great inconvenience to the printer by causing variation in the working of the roller, but soon destroyed the gelatinising power of the glue. The composition then acquired a hard face, which, under the treatment of detergents, broke out into small cracks, often extending over the whole surface of the roller, and rendering it quite useless.

During the last twenty years much improved compositions have been introduced with great success, but the old glue and treacle roller is not yet obsolete. These new compositions do not depend on moisture for maintaining their softness and elasticity, but on fluids that do not volatilise or evaporate. The principal ingredient selected is glycerine, which is a permanent liquid, and will not volatilise or lose bulk under ordinary conditions. Few things in the history of chemical industry are more wonderful than the enormous development of the use of glycerine for manufacturing purposes. A few years ago it was actually thrown away as a waste product—now it is in various ways regarded as one of the most useful if not indispensable materials to be found in the printing office.

The printing of every single sheet of paper, on one side only, by these hand-presses involved no less than nine distinct operations. These were: Inking the roller; inking the forme; laying the sheet on the tympan; flying the frisket and laying it down on the forme; running in the forme under the platen; taking the impression by depressing the platen; running out the forme; lifting the tympan and frisket; releasing the sheet and placing it on the bank. When a sheet of bookwork was printed on both sides, all these operations had to be gone through over again before it was "perfected." As may be expected the process was not only very laborious but very slow. Two men—one pulling and one beating—could produce at a wooden press about 75 impressions per hour. At a Stanhope press, with one man rolling and the other pulling, the output was about 150 to 200 sheets per hour; the Columbian and the Albion presses raised this only slightly—so that 200 per hour was very good work; indeed, even this could not be maintained for long, even when, as was the custom, the men took in turns the two operations. Sheets that had to be printed on both sides were turned out at half the speed named, as a second printing on the back was, of course, necessary. Accordingly one hundred sheets per hour was the largest number that could be printed on the hand presses in use sixty years ago.

CHAPTER V.

THE POWER PRESS—INVENTION OF CYLINDRICAL MACHINE BY KOENIG—THE
FOUR-FEEDER "TIMES" MACHINE OF COWPER AND APPLEGATH—THE
APPLEGATH UPRIGHT ROTARY—HOE'S TYPE-REVOLVING PRESS—THE
WALTER ROTARY WEB MACHINE—INSETTING AND SUPPLEMENT MA-
CHINES—MULTIPLE WEB MACHINES—SPEEDS OF MODERN MACHINES—
APPARATUS FOR BOOKWORK AND GENERAL COMMERCIAL PRINTING.

IT has been mentioned that in 1837 nearly all printing
was done on the hand press. For a few years previously, however, there had been in operation in the
offices of some of the largest book printers and for
printing journals having what was then considered very
large circulations, not presses, but "machines." In these the principle of impression by platen, actuated by screws and levers, was abandoned, and instead of it there was used a revolving metal cylinder, to
squeeze the paper on to the inked type forme. The first apparatus of
the kind was constructed by Frederick Koenig, a German printer, who,
while working at Leipzig was impressed with the idea that the operations
of printing might be simplified and accelerated. He received no en-
couragement in Germany, and came to London in 1806. Thomas Bensley,
a well-known printer, provided him with funds to work out his scheme,
and two other extensive printers afterwards joined the partnership. In
1810 he produced a platen machine. As a printer, he could conceive of nothing better than modifying the methods with which he was accustomed.
It will be seen, in this short sketch of advances made in the art of printing, that the really important improvements—the revolutionary ideas which
have resulted in the marvels of the press of to-day—came, almost without
exception, from men who were not themselves practical and professional

printers. Had they been printers, they would probably have projected nothing better than variations of the apparatus and methods to which they were accustomed. Some years before this a patent for an entirely novel kind of printing had been taken out by William Nicholson, a mechanic and scientific author, but not a printer by trade. He proposed to discard the platen in favour of a cylinder as the pressing surface. This was a project only, for Nicholson never really constructed a machine. Koenig no doubt had this specification brought under his notice. He then gave up the platen idea, and produced a machine in which Nicholson's principle of a cylinder was adopted. Two sheets of a book were printed on this machine in 1812. The remarkable character of the invention reaching the ears of Mr. John Walter, of the "Times," he went to see it, and forthwith ordered a machine to print his newspaper. This machine was completed in 1814, and on the 28th of November of that year a newspaper was for the first time printed by machinery, and by machinery driven by steam.

FREDERICK KOENIG.

It was a double cylinder machine, which printed simultaneouly two copies of a forme of the newspaper on one side only. The feeding was done at the two ends; the inking was effected by providing a vertical cylinder with a hole at the bottom fitted with an air-tight piston, depressed by a screw, which forced the ink out on to two hard rollers, between which it was distributed, and from which it was furnished to the other rollers. The machine printed 1,800 impressions per hour.

The invention of a cylindrical machine, driven from a main shaft and impelled by motive power, was an event of importance second only to that of the invention of printing itself. All modern improvements have their basis in this rotatory apparatus. The hand press, with its nine separate processes involved in the printing of a single sheet could not be much accelerated in its operation. The machine, on the other hand, was

33

subject to no such limitation of output. As will be shown presently, by increasing the number of pressing cylinders and the means of supplying it with paper its capabilities may be almost infinitely increased.

When, in course of time, it was found necessary to improve Koenig's machine, Mr. Walter called in Mr. Edward Cowper, a very eminent professor of mechanics at one of the colleges, who had in 1818 invented several important improvements in printing appliances. Amongst these was a new method of inking, by employing a flat distributing table on which the ink was uniformly spread by rollers having a rotary motion.

EDWARD COWPER.

The ink was conveyed to the table in very small quantities at intervals by a roller which vibrated between a metal roller supplied with ink and the distributing table, to which a small quantity of ink was communicated each time that the vibrating roller touched it. Cowper took away the old inking apparatus from the "Times" machine and put in his own, and in other ways altered and simplified the machine. In 1827 he and his partner, an engineer named Augustus Applegath, constructed a new machine for the journal; and as this was at work when the Queen ascended the throne, a short outline of its arrangements may be of interest. The forme of type was passed backwards and forwards under four cylinders; the machine being supplied with paper from four feeding boards, at each of which a boy stood to supply the sheets. Two boys stood on the floor, and two on a raised platform; four others being placed at the ends of the machine to receive the printed sheets. For the purpose of supplying the sheets to the machine the heap of paper was placed at one end of the feeding board, the boy drawing forward the top sheets by rubbing them or stroking them in with a paper knife. Each sheet was then brought in advance of that below, and the edge of the topmost sheet projected beyond the board and lodged on a wooden roller furnished with tapes which constantly revolved. The roller had no effect on the edge of the sheet until at the proper time a bar was caused to drop, and the paper, caught between two sets of tapes, was carried by them round the cylinder, where it received the impression. The tapes and sheet continued their progress until they arrived at the place where the taker-off stood, and there the tapes separated, and the sheet fell into the hands of the boy. This machine printed at the rate, then regarded as astonishing, of

APPLEGATH MACHINE BUILT FOR THE "TIMES" IN 1848.

4,000 per hour, on one side only. Each sheet, however, was nearly four times the size of the old newspapers printed on Koenig's machine.

This machine really comprised the mechanism of four single machines combined in one frame, all being worked simultaneously by steam as the motive power. It was in use up to 1848, when Augustus Applegath invented an apparatus on altogether new lines. This was regarded as a marvellous mechanical accomplishment; and a machine on the same principles was one of the most popular features of the Great Exhibition of 1851 in

Hyde Park. In the centre of the apparatus, of which an illustration is appended, there was a cylinder about 5½ feet in diameter, which was fixed in a vertical position. The cylinders of printing machines had always previously been placed horizontally, and since this machine was superseded they have always been in the same position. The type was fastened upon the upright cylinder. Around it, as shown in the illustration, were placed eight other vertical cylinders, each about a foot in diameter. They were the paper cylinders, each of which was furnished with a feeding apparatus, whereat one boy laid on the sheets. Necessarily, this feeding apparatus was very peculiar, its object being to convey the sheet from its horizontal position on one of the feeding boards to its vertical position on the paper cylinder. Over each of the eight cylinders was a sloping desk, upon which a stock of unprinted paper was deposited. At the side of the desk stood the layer-on, who pushed the sheets towards the fingers or grippers of the machine. These grippers, seizing upon a sheet, first drew it down in a vertical direction between tapes on the eight vertical frames, until its horizontal edges corresponded with the position of the forme of type on the printing cylinder. Arrived at this position, its vertical motion was stopped by a self-acting apparatus provided in the machine, and it began to move horizontally, and was thus carried towards the printing-cylinder by the tapes. As it passed round this cylinder it was impressed upon the type and printed. It was then carried back horizontally by similar tapes on the other side of the frame, until it arrived at another desk, where the taker-off awaited it. The grippers disengaging it, the taker-off received it and deposited it upon the desk. This movement went on without interruption, and the product was about 9,600 impressions per hour. Inevitable stoppages, however, arising from the number of persons participating in the working of the apparatus, very considerably reduced this nominal speed.

The next step in advance, at the office of the " Times," was the adoption in 1857 of an American press, called the " Type Revolving Printing Machine," manufactured by Col. Richard M. Hoe, of New York. This machine had been introduced into Great Britain in the previous year by the late Mr. Edward Lloyd, for the purpose of printing " Lloyd's Weekly Newspaper." It was not only more compact than the Applegath, but could be driven at a higher rate of speed. The cylinders were horizontal, there being from two to ten impression cylinders, the latter capable of giving nearly 20,000 impressions per hour, on one side of the paper only; but that rate was seldom kept up. One new feature was that the takers-off were dispensed with, by the invention of self-acting "flyers." These deposited the sheets upon tables or flyboards, there being as many of these attached to the machine as there were impression cylinders. At first movable type was used, and it was ingeniously arranged on the larger cylinder. Each column of type was set up on the level, but six or seven columns, for a large newspaper, were nevertheless adjusted side by side. Brass rules of a bevelled shape, or of wedge-like section, were placed

HOE'S TYPE REVOLVING MACHINE.
1857.

between the columns, the bevel varying according to the curvature of the cylinder. All the columns of type were then adjusted and tightened up to occupy, in polygonal fashion, a portion of the circumference of the cylinder, the remaining portion affording space for the inking rollers to act. At a later date stereotype plates, each strictly conforming to the curvature of the cylinder, were used on the Hoe machine, with a great increase of speed and economy.

Up to this time single sheets of paper had alone been used. These limited most effectively the output of the printing machine, because one man could not feed in more than 1,000 sheets per hour—and, indeed, few men did as much. The only means of increasing the rate of printing was by multiplying the number of impression cylinders to which the paper was fed. When these were more than six in number the complication became great, the stoppages frequent, the waste considerable, the risk of accidents serious, and the cost of the work heavy.

An entirely new era was now about to commence. In 1862, Mr. John Walter, like his predecessors, ever on the look-out for improved mechanical means of production, caused experiments to be made having two objects in view—to print from a continuous roll of paper, which could be fed in automatically at any speed at which the printing cylinder could be driven,

JOHN WALTER.

and to print both sides of the paper at once. The experiments were carried on during the six years between 1862 and 1868, and at last one machine was finished. Three more were completed by the end of 1869, when the edition of the journal was printed on them in less than half the time previously occupied, with one-fifth of the hands required for the Hoe machines, and with a much less waste of paper and other materials. Only three men were required in the actual working; one to start and stop the machine, and two to attend to the delivery of the sheets, which came out flat.

The merit of having first completed a practical rotary machine, is due to William Bullock, an engineer of Philadelphia, U.S.A., whose first press was finished in 1865, after years of patient experiment. The inventor did not long enjoy the fruits of his labours, for he was accidentally killed while testing one of his machines, in 1868. The "Daily Telegraph" had a Bullock web machine at work before the Walter press was in operation.

The next improvement which requires to be mentioned here is the invention of the " Supplement " press, manufactured by Messrs. Hoe and Co., of New York and London. It prints a journal of variable sizes, of 8, 10, 12, 16, 20, or 24 pages; it cuts the sheets, fits them together, and folds them, and finally delivers them on the receiver counted into quires of 27 copies, or any number that may be desired. The illustration shows a cartload of reels of paper on the road to the printing office. This has now become quite an ordinary sight in London, and is passed by in the

THE WALTER PRESS.

street without remark. It is a great contrast to the old plan of delivering the paper in reams; and, simple though it seems, marks the climax of a long series of mechanical successes in the paper mill, as well as in the printing office.

When the paper is delivered it is quite dry, and as it receives the ink from the plates in the printing process best when it is somewhat damp, it has to be passed through a wetting machine. The reel, as it goes through this machine, is pressed against an iron cylinder, which dips into a trough of water, and thus the paper is damped. In the engraving one reel of

DELIVERY OF PAPER IN REELS.

paper is nearly finished wetting. The man is standing against the wetted reel, which is growing bigger and bigger as the dry reel at the rear end of the machine is growing smaller and smaller. The reel, which may be about six feet wide and four miles in length, has to be lifted on to and off the machine by means of the crane, as it is far too heavy to move anyhow else, weighing nearly three-quarters of a ton.

REEL DAMPING MACHINE.

The Hoe Double Supplement Press is capable of printing, cutting, and folding 24,000 copies per hour of a full-sized newspaper of eight, ten, or more pages. The main reel is shown on the left hand of the illustration ; it is 75 inches wide and 36 inches in diameter. The supplement reel, 37½ inches wide, is on the right hand. The plates on the main part of the press are not visible in the drawing, but those for the supplement portion are shown, in cylindrical form, parallel to the spindle of the supplement reel, but on the level of the head of the attendant. The stereo plates are first attached to two large cylinders, and if there is an enlarged paper the plates for

HOE SUPPLEMENT PRESS, PRESENT DAY.

these are put on the supplement portion. The chief reel of paper is suspended close to the floor and fed into the machine between the face of the stereotype plates and the impression cylinder covered with blanket. The first cylinder prints it on one side, and it is conveyed to the next, which prints it on the other. The ink fountain is placed over the large cylinder, and is surrounded by rollers of varying size up to six inches in diameter, which distribute it on to the inking rollers. The cylinders bearing the plates revolve 200 times every minute. The paper is printed before it is cut up. It is passed upwards and over rollers at the top of the machine, and as it goes, a revolving knife presses upon it at right angles with the width and divides it into two longitudinal lengths. These two sheets then pass over bars, which turn them at right angles to their original direction, and they immediately meet the supplement sheet coming from its own part of the machine, which passes in between the two main sheets. Supplement and twin lengths are carried together over and down the outer surface of the sloping triangular steel plate, or "former," with the apex at the bottom. The sheets curl over and under the edges of the "former," until they are drawn together in the proper order of their numbered pages between a pair of horizontal rollers. Still the length of these sheets remains connected with the web as it unrolls. Now, however, the whole set of pages encounter cylinders armed with knives with a saw-like edge, sheathed in indiarubber beds, which separate the connection, while the folding blade of a cylinder opposite creases down the middle between the pages. The latter then pass through small rollers that fold over the papers on the line of the crease, and the newspaper is finished. A rotary fly deposits the papers on to a set of leather bands, which are continuously travelling forward, and on which the papers rapidly accumulate —a gap between every 27 copies denoting a quire. The engraving shows the method of clearing away the folded papers from the delivery part of the machine.

CLEARING THE DELIVERY.

There are several other kinds of supplement machines made by various makers. Amongst these may be mentioned the Victory machine on which many newspapers of large circulation are printed. It was the inventor of this machine, the late Mr. G. A. Wilson, who, in 1870, first added a folding apparatus, which turned out the copies ready for sale by the newsagents. A first-class web machine of the present day will print and fold four and six-page papers at the rate of 48,000 copies per hour; eight, ten, and twelve-page papers at the rate of 24,000 copies per hour; and sixteen, twenty, or twenty-four-page papers at the rate of 12,000 per hour—all cut at the head, and counted in bundles of any number required. Such machines are arranged for three independent rolls of paper, each roll having its own complete printing mechanism. One of the most popular weeklies is printed at the highest rate of speed on a machine of this kind, which, besides folding the paper into quarto pages, puts on the wrappers, and wire-stitches them.

Bookwork, including periodical work, was done, in the year 1837 on Applegath and Cowper's Perfecting Machine, the general features of which have already been indicated. There were then, however, very few offices

THE APPLEGATH & COWPER MACHINE.

indeed which required such a costly apparatus. This style of printing was almost entirely restricted to the hand press, mainly for two reasons. When editions were small it was cheapest to print them at press. There was, too, in existence a general prejudice against machine work. It was thought that fine printing could not be obtained by the employment of the cylinder principle, and that the platen was the only expedient that would give satisfactory results. In view of the many imperfections of the machines of sixty years ago, this objection to them was to a certain extent well founded. It has now entirely disappeared. The very finest "art" work is produced on cylinder machines, and with a cleanness of impression, solidity, and brilliancy, accuracy of register, and uniformity of colour that no hand press could possibly accomplish. Certain classes of printing, such as that of process blocks, could not be done at all on a press, because the requisite strength of impression could not possibly be obtained from it. Jobbing printing, too, is now almost invariably produced by machine. There are two kinds of machines for doing this kind of work. One is a cylinder machine, in which the type forme is placed on a flat bed, on a carriage which travels backward and forward. At one point in its journey it receives the ink from composition rollers, and at another it is brought, with the paper on the top of it, under the pressure of the cylinder. There are elaborate mechanical arrangements for ensuring a regulated supply of ink to the rollers, and giving a firm unshrinking pressure on the types. The other class of machine is known as the small platen machine. The platen and the type forme are in a vertical position perfectly parallel to each other at the time of impression. The paper being fed in between them, they are brought gradually together, and their degree of proximity is so regulated that the platen gives a quick but perfectly solid impact upon the forme. The attendant simply lays on and takes off the sheet; all the rest is done automatically. Some presses of this kind have a mechanical delivery, so that feeding them is all that is necessary.

CHAPTER VI.

THE WORK OF THE COMPOSITOR—PROJECTS FOR SUPERSEDING IT—TYPE-SET-
TING MACHINES—THEIR LIMITED SUCCESS—TYPOGRAPHY WITHOUT
TYPES.

IN the preceding chapters it has been shown that during the last sixty years the impression department—what is called in the trade the machine-room department—has been completely revolutionised by the introduction of more rapid appliances and better processes.   Up to within half-a-dozen years ago, however, the other department—that of the composing-room—was conducted on the same plan and furnished with the same tools as in 1837.

This remarkable state of things has not continued because no efforts have been made to change it.   On the contrary, during the last fifty years hundreds of patents have been taken out for apparatus designed to compose types.   Immense sums of money have been expended in efforts to carry out these patents.   Printers have invested large sums of money in buying type-setting machines.   One or two of our greatest printing firms have spent thousands of pounds upon inventions of this character, now entirely discarded.   As early as 1822 an American engineer, Dr. William Church, patented in Great Britain certain printing machines and other inventions relating to printing.   The "machine" was merely a modification of the Stanhope press, but the other inventions were strikingly original. The principal object in view was, as stated in Hansard's "Typographia," to print constantly from new type, which end was proposed to be effected by simplifying the processes of casting, composing, and distributing. The type was to be delivered perfect by machinery, and laid, as it was cast, with unerring order and exactness in separate compartments. The compositor's work was then to be effected by other apparatus directed by keys like those of an organ. Thus was the type to be arranged in words and lines as quickly as in the performance of music; to be all perfectly correct, as no error was to be possible, except one arising from striking the wrong key. It was claimed to be less expensive under this

HAND COMPOSING-ROOM.

system of type-founding to melt the type and re-cast it than to perform the tedious operation of distribution. It was calculated that two men could produce 75,000 new types per hour, and in composing one man was to perform as much as three or four compositors. In the production of types the saving, so printers were told, was ninety-nine parts in a hundred, and in the composition, distribution, and reading, three parts in four.

Dr. Church is not recorded to have actually made a machine according to this specification. He anticipated, however, principles which in after years were destined to be extensively worked out. No other proposal than this for mechanical type-setting was in existence when the Queen came to the throne. The only idea suggested for accelerating the setting up of type matter was to use logotypes—that is, pieces of metal bearing on their edge in relief, not a single letter, but several, such as "and," "ing," and so on. It was thought that if the compositor had to make one lift only for three or four letters, his output would be considerably increased. The plan—a printer's idea, by the way—proved to be a perfect failure. In 1840 a French inventor, Gaubert, devised a plan of sorting types, so to speak, by giving them various notches, which could be discriminated by a machine, and thus allow of automatic distribution. It

YOUNG AND DELCAMBRE'S COMPOSING MACHINE.

was in 1842 that the first machine for composing types was really used in an English composing-room. This machine, patented two years previously, was invented by Young and Delcambre —neither of whom was a printer. It seems strange to learn that the well-known periodical, the "Family Herald," was started to give this machine employment. This fact is mentioned by Mr. J. F. Wilson in his "Recollections of an Old Printer" (London, 1896). The apparatus was a huge failure, but the periodical was a great success.

Many composing machines have been since constructed on the same principle as Young and Delcambre's. The operator, shown to the right in the engraving, depressed successively the keys arranged on a key-board something like that of a piano. The types had been arranged in rows— one sort in one row. These rows were laid side by side, in grooves or tubes, the outlets of which were ranged in a line. On a key being depressed by the operator, the first letter in any one of the groups or tubes was extracted. It was drawn or fell out. It had next to be led through channels to be conveyed to another part of the mechanism. The channels, it will be seen, all converged to one point—a kind of spout. Successive letters were extracted from their receptacles in the same way, forming words. A space was placed between these. The composed matter emerged from the composing machine in a line of indefinite length, and it had to be divided into shorter lines, all of them of identical length—that of the width of the column, if the matter was for a newspaper, or of the page, if it was for a book. This operation of making the lines of a regulated length is called justifying. It involves, if the compositor has not to suspend his work from time to time, the employment of a second operator.

The channels, through which the types were led, one after another, to the place where they were assembled together, as in the "stick" of the hand compositor, were cut into a piece of metal called the guide plate. The great majority of machines still made are on this guide-plate principle. In the accompanying illustration the operation of justifying is shown. On the left is the distributing apparatus, whereby the types, after they were printed, were returned to the supply grooves, from whence they were taken

DISTRIBUTING AND JUSTIFYING.

to the first machine—the composing apparatus—to be again re-set.

This arrangement is undoubtedly ingenious, but it has been found to be far from satisfactory. The converging grooves in a machine of this class have to be adapted for types of different thicknesses being brought down one channel. There is a much greater variety in the width of letters of the same alphabet than most people, except type-founders, suppose. We all know that an "m" is wider than an "n," but the niceties of difference between some of the other letters could only be detected by the use of delicate gauges. The arrangements of the guide plate sometimes consist of fine springs, which, with rough handling of any sort, get out of order. They are very susceptible to wear, and very liable to disarrangement. Again, letters are of very diverse weights, and they have a tendency to fall with unequal velocity. Sometimes they strike the receiving portion and rebound; sometimes they turn round unexpectedly in their channels; sometimes they stick fast and have to be released with a bodkin. The dust and particles which often adhere to the grooves, as well as to the types, render their delivery uncertain. Hence the most perfect cleanliness of the guide plate and of the type is essential. Much time is required to properly clean the guide plate, and in the printing office unclean and sticky type cannot always be avoided. In working type that is not entirely clean the dirt is left on the plate in specks and little heaps. These cause obstructions, and the letters are turned in their course. The objection is of more importance than might at first be imagined. It is not felt so much on dry as on damp days. It has been said that type-setting machines work better in some parts of America than in England, because there the atmosphere is dryer. Possibly there is some truth in this; at any rate, the difficulty arising from such a small cause as insufficiently cleansed type, and a damp guide plate, illustrates the extreme delicacy of such machines—which is one of the chief drawbacks in using them. Again, the types are not always delivered in the receiver in the proper order. This may arise from the operator depressing the keys at a faster rate than the types can be conveyed down the guide plate. Sometimes, too, the types are brought down to the receiver faster than they can be cleared aside for successive letters. The claim that some machines are capable of being operated at any speed at which the keys can be touched is certainly not corroborated by experience.

The Young and Delcambre machine has long since been discarded, but many subsequent inventions have, as above mentioned, been based on

MACKIE COMPOSING MACHINE.

it. These may be distinguished by their adoption of the guide plate expedient; the setting of the matter in the long line, involving the second operator; and the use of a subsidiary machine for distributing the type, requiring a third person to look after it.

Another principle, entirely different to that of the guide plate one, has, however, been adopted by makers of type-setting machines. This is known as the rotary system—of which the Mackie machine, depicted in the illustration, was one of the most interesting examples. This was completed about 1858, and was the invention of a journalist of Warrington—Dr. Alex. Mackie. Instead of the types being arranged in tubes, which sloped towards the point of delivery, they were contained upon a revolving horizontal disc, and were by the revolving of this disc, which was somewhat like a carriage wheel, brought to the receiver. The Mackie machine has now been altogether superseded; but there are a few machines by other inventors still in use which embody the rotary principle, with the variation that the type receptacles are not fixed on a horizontal revolving disc, but consist of grooves in a kind of revolving vertical pillar. Such machines are capable of being worked at a much higher rate of speed than the guide plate machines. The drawback is their liability to cause a great deal of damage to type. If they are not perfectly adjusted, kept in a proper state of repair, and worked by the most careful, experienced, and circumspect operators, they may break from time to time a very considerable weight of type. This item of breakage greatly detracts from—if it does not altogether neutralise—the economic advantages that are claimed for machine type-setting. Even if the type is not broken, it may be worn unduly. The edges are often rounded by frequent passage through grooves. The wear especially occurs to the feet of the type, and one result is that they go " off their feet," and occasion a variety of troubles which all printers can appreciate.

It would have been gratifying to chronicle the fact that type-setting machines, considering their great ingenuity and the immense labour and expense that have been devoted to making and introducing them, had been as successful as printing machines ; but such is not the fact. Their use is extremely limited, and is becoming less and less. They are so delicate and so complicated that they are very expensive ; and their expensiveness does not end with their first cost. It is largely increased by the percentage which has to be allowed for repairs and for breakage of type. A machine, with its auxiliary distributor, costs from £350 to £500 and upwards. As a rule, only one size and face of type can be advantageously composed with it. Now, a book printer generally uses ten or more sizes or styles of book-type in his work. The cost of buying an equal number of machines would be very great, if not prohibitory. If a machine of this kind is to be even moderately remunerative, it must be kept constantly running, but there are few offices comparatively in which machines could be kept going without a stoppage for copy or letter. When they are idle the loss is heavy, not only in regard to the capital invested in them, but the waste of time of the operator. In hand-composing a man may have, during one day, to work from half-a-dozen different pairs of cases, and no time is lost in changing from one to ·the other ; but when machines are used, every change is a loss. The cost of running machines and the high rates of wages demanded by skilled operators, is another drawback to any machine which cannot be safely depended upon to compose a large quantity of type within a given space of time.

The prices at which printing is done have been enormously reduced during the last half-century, and this has been rendered possible, not by reducing wages—for they have increased—but by the adoption of labour-saving machinery. As has been already mentioned, up to 1837 nearly all printing was done on the hand press; yet now there is hardly an office in the kingdom in which the press-work is not done by machine. Nevertheless types are set now as they were sixty, a hundred, four hundred years ago.

AN UNWELCOME INTRUDER.

A type-setting machine of any kind is not to be found in even as many as two hundred out of the ten thousand printing offices existing in the United Kingdom. The consensus of opinion on the part of printers is distinctly unfavourable to such machines. It is recognised that, although for certain classes of work, and under certain conditions, one or other of these machines may be to a certain extent satisfactory in their results, ordinary type composition is done quite as cheaply—and much more conveniently—by hand as by machine. For many years the incursion of the type-setting machine into the printing office was the compositor's bugbear —as George Cruickshank so humorously pictured. But the dreaded visitor did not do much harm—it hardly came to stay. It frightfully alarmed the timorous type-lifter, who feared that his occupation would soon be gone; and then it slowly retreated by another door, and the result is that the compositor goes on just as he ever did. If, however, type-composing machines have effected so little change in the conditions of the printing business, quite another style of composing machine has already brought about the most remarkable results, as will be now briefly pointed out.

COMPOSING THE "DAILY TELEGRAPH."

Anyone who is privileged to visit the composing-rooms of hundreds of first-class journals in town and country, will find that type-setting has been almost entirely done away with. Instead of the long rows of frames, with their desk-like tops holding cases, as shown in a preceding illustration, he will perceive a series of machines such as are depicted in the accompanying engraving. One operator sits in front of each of them. His copy is fixed in a convenient position before him, he reads it, and begins to tap the keys of the key-board in front of his seat. Within a minute or two there

THE LINOTYPE COMPOSING MACHINE.

is seen emerging from the machine a bright metal bar, which, on being examined, will be found to present on its edge a line of reading matter—the exact equivalent to a line of type, as far as the printed impression it makes is concerned. Once started, successive bars are ejected from the machine with extraordinary regularity and rapidity. These are collected on a galley, like lines of movable type, and they go finally to be stereotyped precisely as type matter is stereotyped. The operator taps the key, the machine does all the rest. And here comes in the wonderful advantage derived from the transformation of the scene in the composing-room. Each operator produces from six to eight or ten times as much composed matter as any type-setter could achieve, and does it without type. Within the five square feet which he and his apparatus occupy, there is as much composition executed as could be obtained from frames and cases occupying more than as many yards.

This apparatus is known as the Linotype machine—a word whose derivation is tolerably obvious. Remembering that it makes its own type—or rather, does without it, which is quite as good, if not much better—that it composes and distributes, that its operator is his own type-founder, his own compositor, and his own distributor, it may justly be regarded as the greatest mechanical marvel of the last sixty years. Indeed, it would be right to go much further than that, and to say that it is the first really great improvement in typography—apart from the printing machines we have already mentioned—since John Gutenberg, the discoverer of letter-press printing, invented the mould and the matrix whereby he produced movable interchangeable types capable of combination and re-combination to an unlimited extent, and which formed the really fundamental principle upon which typography itself was based.

This wonderful result is effected by a machine of multitudinous parts—nearly two thousand separate pieces of metal, in all the shapes known to engineers—but one which is, nevertheless, remarkably free from complexity. Indeed, the manner in which it does its work may be understood readily by anyone possessing the smallest modicum of mechanical information. The product of the Linotype apparatus is a bar, like that shown in the engraving. The length of the bar may be varied at will; for instance, the longest lines in this brochure are set to a measure of 30 ems Pica,

A LINOTYPE BAR.

which is equivalent to five inches, while smaller ones are only 15 ems long. These, and a variety of other sizes, are set by the same machine. The height of the bar is precisely that of an ordinary type. The width is that of the fount to which the bar corresponds; in this case it is Small Pica, which is one-seventh of an inch. The bar is cast in a mould, one face of which is formed of a line of matrices, shaped as in the illus-

LINOTYPE
MATRIX.

tration. On the front of the matrix is cut a letter or other character in intaglio; that is, it is sunk. The cast from this is, of course, in relief—like the face of ordinary types—the raised surfaces of which receive the printing ink, which, by the pressure of the printing machine is transferred to the paper. It is not proposed here to go into mechanical details, which would be tedious and perhaps unintelligible were they unaccompaned by sectional diagrams. Each touch of the operator on the key-board releases a matrix from the place where it is stored. The matrix runs rapidly but orderly down a channel until it comes in contact with an endless band. This conveys it to a contrivance which pushes it into its proper position in the assembly-box. The latter corresponds to the ordinary compositor's stick, for in it are set up all the characters for the line, only they are matrices and not types. Now, before a compositor can give his line that minutely accurate width which is imperative, he has to spend a certain amount of time in justifying—that is, in putting in more space betwen the words or taking some out, yet leaving all of them with a fairly equal distance between each other. He has for the moment to stop picking up his types, and this accounts for a good deal—perhaps one-sixth—of the time occupied in producing a given piece of composed matter. The linotypist is troubled with no such interruption. He has already placed between each of his words as they were composed a double wedge of steel, the end of which hangs below the level of the matrix. A touch on a lever actuates mechanism whereby the wedge is sent up, becoming wider as it moves, and the exact width of the space—and of all the spaces in the line—is thus automatically determined, and provided for with absolute accuracy and absolutely instantaneously. The line being justified, is now ready to be cast. A metal-pot containing molten metal is provided, and a mechanical mould, whereby the metal is injected into the sunken parts of the matrix. The bar is thus formed, and requires only to be trimmed at the bottom and at the side to make it range evenly with a line of ordinary type. Bar after bar is thus formed with the greatest rapidity, and each is pushed forward on to a galley, whence it is taken to be made up.

Now, if this bar, which is in reality of the nature of a stereotype, had been cast from movable types, each of these would have had to be separately replaced in the case. Hence would arise the necessity for another time-consuming operation—that of distribution. Distributing may occupy the compositor about one-third of the time that he was engaged in setting the matter. To put it in another way: Suppose he is paid for setting one thousand letters the sum of sixpence. Out of that he will have spent one-penny's worth of time in justifying, and two-penny worth in distributing—so that threepence is the nett price of the actual composing. But the Linotype machine calls for no help whatever in distributing or replacing its matrices. The line is carried up and the spaces dropped out. The matrices are hung upon a bar of peculiar shape, having projections which, in conjunction with the little steps like the wards of a key, shown in the block of a matrix, suspend them until they are over their own proper receptacles, when, the support being withdrawn, they simply drop into their places in due order, ready to be re-used in the formation of another linotype.

The working conditions of the compositor have been vastly improved by the introduction of this beautiful machine. No greater contrast could be imagined than that between the irksome labour of the old-fashioned type-setter and the cheerful, intelligent work of the modern linotype operator. The former stood at his case nearly the whole of the live-long day. The latter works seated. The one had his left hand per-petually occupied in holding his metal "stick," and the fingers of the other employed travelling around the boxes, picking out the ofttimes dirty and dusty types, adjusting them in his stick, and stopping every now and then to justify. The other merely watches his copy and taps his keys with a finger of either or of both hands. The two pictures need not be elaborated; every printer knows the tediousness and the monotony of the old system of type-setting.

But the Linotype has not been brought into our printing offices merely to ameliorate the lot of the compositor—excellent as such an object would undoubtedly be. The machine has as its prime object the production of composition—in every respect as good as any other kind of composition, and at a speed which without the machine would be absolutely unattainable, but, above all, to reduce the cost of this composition. This saving in wages, in wear and tear, in rent of floor space, and in other ways, is from thirty to fifty per cent. This is an absolute fact—demonstrated by newspaper managers all over the kingdom. And this is not obtained by employing cheap labour; on the contrary, the new operator is paid from twenty to fifty per cent. for his time more than the old type-lifter. His work is not only more pleasant; it is more profitable to him, and it is more profitable to his employer. The machine operator accordingly is, as a rule, a far more contented, more intelligent, and more dependable man than he of the movable types a generation ago. The machine has unquestionably elevated the condition of the working printer, and in doing this has raised the tone of the composing-room. Moral as well as hygienic conditions have been completely altered of late years. The pallid, wearied "comp,"—with "his nose in the space-box" for eight or nine hours a day; with his frequent over-indulgence in stimulants, distinctly attributable to the fatiguing nature of his calling; his weak chest and chronic cough (ninety per cent. of the old hand-compositors died from pulmonary complaints caused by their constant stooping over their cases)—all these are things of the past. Amidst the many improvements in industrial life which have obtained during the reign of our Queen, these changes in the conditions of the printing office are amongst the most beneficent, as undoubtedly they are amongst the most conspicuous.

It is not alone the printers—masters and workpeople—that are benefiting by these changes. The public are very much concerned in them indeed. Day after day we get a splendidly-printed sixteen-page morning paper for a penny; an equally well printed eight-page evening paper for a half-penny. Such issues as these were never attempted in the pre-Linotype days. It is not to be asserted that all the credit is due to the composing machine; as shown elsewhere, cheap paper and cheap methods of printing have done much to render such things possible. But the fact remains that they were never attempted before. Again, a large number of books are also set up on this machine, and some of them are sold to the public at astoundingly low prices. To say the least, the cheapness of their composition has been one element in the result. In the near future we may have even bigger papers and a larger number of cheap books. Surely these are boons to the public—advances which go to spread even still more widely than at present education, intelligence, and morality amongst Her Majesty's loyal subjects. As Mr. W. E. Gladstone declared on being shown a Linotype machine, "It is a machine from which I cannot but anticipate effects equally extensive and beneficent to mankind."

CHAPTER VII.✿✿✿✿✿✿

TYPE-FOUNDING—THE HAND METHOD—INVENTION OF TYPE-CASTING MACHINE—CHANGES IN FASHION IN TYPE FACES.

LL the type produced in this country in 1837 was cast in the hand mould. In a pamphlet published in 1839, giving an account of a visit to Messrs. Clowes's establishment in Stamford Street, there is a graphic description of the scene in the foundry, and it is applicable to nearly all the foundries of the period. The visitor saw a number of workmen in paper caps and with their shirt sleeves tucked up, in front of a long table, or sitting at another table in the middle of the room—"intently occupied at some sort of minute sniggling operation." What wholly engrossed the first attention of the stranger was the extraordinary convulsive attitudes of ten men who appeared as if they were all possessed with St. Vitus's dance, or as if they were performing some druidical or dervishical religious ceremony. These men were casting the types, and the writer describes their method and their tools. "In the centre of a three-inch cube of hard wood, which is split into halves,

TYPE-CASTING IN 1837.

there is inserted the copper matrix of the letter to be cast. Down the line of junction of the two halves there is pierced from the outer face of the wood to the matrix, a small hole into which the liquid metal was poured, and from which it could be extracted by opening the cube." The type-caster was provided with a little furnace and a small cauldron of liquid metal. At his feet was a small heap of coals. His ladles were of various denominations, according to the type to be cast—varying from one which held a quarter of a pound of metal, to the smaller, but much more frequently used one, which held about as much as would go inside a small hazel nut. With the mould in his left hand, the founder with his right dipped his little ladle into the metal, instantly poured the metal into the hole of the cube, and then, in order to force it down to the matrix, he jerked up the mould higher than his head. As suddenly he lowered it, and by a quick movement opened it, shook out the type, closed the mould, re-filled it, re-jerked it in the air, re-opened it, and by a repetition of these manœuvres each workman produced from 400 to 500 types per hour. By the convulsive jerk the liquid was unavoidably tossed about in various directions, yet the type-founder performed the scalding operation with naked arms, evidently in many places bearing the marks of severe burns.

As soon as a sufficient heap of type was cast, it was placed "before an intelligent little boy, whose pale wan face sufficiently explained the effect that had been produced upon it by the antimony of the metal." He broke off the jet of metal left on the foot of the type; and it is observed as an incident of the occupation: "by handling new types a workman has been known to lose his thumb and fore-finger." By a third process the types were rubbed on a flat stone, which took off the roughness or "burr" from their sides. By a fourth process the types were set in a long com-posing-stick, with their nicks uppermost; and by a fifth process the bottom extremities were smoothed by the plane. The last operation was telling them down and papering them up.

This primitive process was for many years maintained with stolid pertinacity. All proposals for improvement were at once discountenanced by the type-founders of the day, who being few in number had a very good understanding amongst themselves, and they were strong enough, and wealthy enough, to crush any attempt to introduce machinery into the business. In the reports of the juries of the Great Exhibition of 1851, it is related that some years previously Louis John Pouchée took out patents for Great Britain for a machine for casting type whereby, it was claimed, about 200 types could be cast at one operation, and the casting operation repeated twice in a minute, or even quicker. Like many other pioneers of mechanical progress, Pouchée got into difficulties, and had to dispose of his invention. The type-founders formed a syndicate for its purchase, at the modest price of £100. They employed a printer in Covent Garden to negotiate with Pouchée, who probably would not have sold his machine if he had known who was in reality endeavouring to buy it. The transaction was completed, and the machine soon found its way to the leading foundry of the day. It was not to be worked, but to be simply destroyed. The son of Pouchée wrote to one of the technical journals recording with what deliberation and care, lest any trace should remain, the founders destroyed the machine. They had taken it out to sea, and thrown it overboard.

Abroad, type-founding was done on a large scale by more or less automatic machines. These machines were not allowed to be worked in this country. It may be wondered at that some enterprising individual did not buy a type-casting machine and start in business in opposition to the founders. This, however, was impracticable, for this reason: a type-casting machine was of no use without a stock of matrices. These matrices were made by each foundry exclusively for its own use. The artisans who had been trained to make them were few in number. Theirs was a very delicate and highly skilful kind of work, which required years of apprenticeship to learn. The principle of division of labour was carried out to the utmost; each man was acquainted with only a part, and generally a minute part, of the type-founder's art. Then, again, the making of the matrices was very costly. Immense sums would have had to be spent to collect a stock of matrices such as existing foundries possessed, as the result of long years of trading. The type-founding firms were few in number—in England and Scotland some half-dozen, all told. They had the business securely in their own hands, and were able to defy competition.

This was not, however, to last for ever. In 1838 David Bruce, of New York, invented a thoroughly successful casting machine. It was almost automatic in its action, and could be worked by hand or power. The metal was projected into the mould by a pump, the spout of which was in front of the metal pot. The mould was movable, and at every revolution of the crank, it came up to the spout, received a charge of metal, and flew back with a fully-formed type in its interior. The upper half of the mould lifted, and the type was ejected at the rate of 100 to 175 per minute; or about 6,000 per hour, as compared with the 400 per hour of the hand caster.

This American machine, although invented in 1838, and largely employed in many American and Continental foundries, was not introduced into Great Britain until about the year 1848, and then in a very tentative fashion. Before long, however, the prejudice against improvement had to give way, and machines were eventually found in every foundry.

ROOM IN A MODERN TYPE-FOUNDRY.

Bruce's machine has since been modified in details, but his principle is the one upon which all subsequent machines were constructed, with a single exception. That was the invention, in 1862, of Mr. J. R. Johnson, a chemist—not a type-founder—of a machine which not only cast the type but rubbed and dressed it, and removed the break or jet. The metal was poured in at one end of the machine and came out at the other end in the shape of type fit for immediate use by the printer. This machine also has since been improved in its minor parts.

The art of type-founding was in as backward a state artistically in 1837 as mechanically. At the risk of disfiguring our pages we reproduce a few of the most widely used so-called "ornamental" types then supplied by the founders. These hideous distortions of the Roman form were in use up till twenty years ago. Shortly after then, there were brought over from America and Germany a number of founts, which were elegant and diversified in style, and were a complete contrast to the abortions previously supplied by the English founders. These have improved the taste of printers and printers' customers, and native founders have had to emulate them. The result is seen in the very beautiful specimens of jobbing work now so generally produced.

The Roman types of 1837 were certainly more pleasing, but they were tame, formal, and harsh. Above all, they were deficient in legibility— the cardinal virtue in types intended for books. They were designed in the style of the Italian printer, Bodoni, and their characteristics were heavy body lines and extremely fine hair lines. The little horizontal lines, called the serifs, were flat, very fine, and they easily broke off, giving the type a very unprepossessing appearance. This style is called the "modern face."

In 1843 Pickering, the publisher, wanted to print a book in the style of type used by the printers of the seventeenth and part of the eighteenth

EUROPE.

ENGLAND.

SCOTLAND IRELAND

LONDON.

EDINBURGH.

DUBLIN.

WALES.

MANCHESTER.

"ORNAMENTAL" TYPES OF 1837.

Quousque tandem abutere, Catilina, patientia nostra? quamdiu nos etiam furor iste tuus eludet? quem ad finem sese effrenata jactabit audacia? nihilne te nocturnum præsidium palatii, nihil urbis vigiliæ, nihil timor populi, nihil consensus bonorum omnium, nihil hic munitissimus habendi senatus locus, nihil horum ora vultusque moverunt? patere tua consilia non sentis? constrictam jam omnium horum conscientia teneri conjurationem tuam non vides? quid proxima, quid superiore nocte egeris, ubi fueris, quos convocaveris, quid consilii ceperis, quem nostrum ignorare arbitraris? O tempora, o mores! Senatus hoc intelligit, consul videt: hic tamen vivit. &c.

ROMAN STYLE OF 1837.

centuries. He induced his printer, Whittingham, of the Chiswick Press, to go to the oldest English foundry in existence—the Caslon Foundry—to ascertain whether there were any matrices in existence from which types of the required style could be cast. Happily a number of punches of Caslon I. had been preserved, though without the slightest expectation of their ever again being brought into requisition. The firm consented to supply a fount of this type, and there was soon such a call for it that an entire series was produced. The demand induced other founders to cut founts presenting the characteristics of the old style, and these have ever since maintained their popularity.

RESPECTING their interior polity, our colonies are properly of thefe three forts 1. Provincial eftablifhments, the confti-tutions of which will depend on their refpective commiffions iffued by the crown to the governor and the inftructions which ufually accompany all commiffions; under the authority of which their provincial affemblies are conftituted, with power

ORIGINAL CASLON FACE REVIVED IN 1837.

The specimen annexed is reproduced from the magnificent volume of Specimens of the Original Caslon Old Face, issued during the present year under the auspices of Mr. Thomas W. Smith, the present principal proprietor of the historic Caslon Foundry

Space here is too limited to admit of reference to more recent changes in type fashions, with one exception: the Kelmscott Press type of the late William Morris, and of which we present a specimen. These types

KELMSCOTT PRESS.

Secretary: H. Halliday Sparling, 8, Hammersmith Terrace, London, W.

SIDONIA THE SORCERESS, translated from the German of William Meinhold, by Francesca Speranza, Lady Wilde. In one volume, quarto, 456 pages, in Golden type, with borders, flowered letters, and other ornaments. In black and red. 300 to be printed. 10 on vellum. To be published by William Morris, at Four Guineas, bound in vellum of extra quality, with silk ties.

are designed on the styles favoured by the early Venetian printers, es-pecially of Nicholas Jenson. Mr. Morris designed his own founts, and the types were cast for him at the Fann Street Foundry of Sir Charles Reed's Sons. Several other private presses have since arisen, and these, too, have had founts designed specially for their own use.

Type-founding is no longer a mystery. Hundreds of printing offices now possess their own type-casting machines. The manufacture of these has become a special branch of the engineering trade. Matrices can be readily bought; there is no secrecy as to their production now. Many of them are not cut by the old, laborious, slow method; they are electro-typed at a trifling cost. The beautiful faces of the Linotype founts are cast from matrices made from originals produced by a machine of recent invention, the sole use of which is in the hands of the Linotype Company. As this plan can be applied not only to body founts, such as romans used in books and newspapers, but to fancy founts of the most delicate and beautiful kinds, it may ere long quite revolutionise the art of the punch-cutter, and introduce many much-needed improvements into the type-founding business itself.

CHAPTER VIII.

STEREOTYPING—THE PLASTER AND THE PAPER PROCESS—APPLICATION TO BOOK AND NEWS WORK—ELECTROTYPING.

ONE of the arts auxiliary to printing have made more progress than that of stereotyping. The fact may be attributed to the demand for the extremely fast production of copies of newspapers. Stereotyping permits of the production of almost any number of replicas of a letterpress surface, and these may be printed simultaneously at different machines. The fast machines of the present day are all rotaries, the cylinders of which are clothed with curved plates. The system of rotary printing, except to the extent that it was, in a rudimentary form, carried on when the type-revolving press was in use, would be almost impossible without a method of casting cylindrical stereo plates. Other considerations would go to show, not only the advantages economical and mechanical of the art, but its absolute necessity as an adjunct of modern press work.

The history of stereotyping commences as far back as the year 1725, when an Edinburgh goldsmith, William Ged, cast some plates very imperfectly for the University of Cambridge. His purpose and progress were impeded by the prejudices of both compositors and pressmen. On his death. in 1749, his son, James Ged, proposed to carry on the business, but was unable to do so for want of funds; and stereotyping was abandoned for nearly thirty years. Andrew Tilloch re-invented it, not having heard of Ged's system, and took out a patent in partnership with Foulis, printer to the University of Glasgow, in the year 1784. About 1797 Professor Wilson made some improvements in the system; but up to 1800 the art, although it had been twice invented and practised, had fallen into disuse, and might be said to have become unknown. Earl Stanhope, who has been mentioned in connection with the iron press which bears his name, recognised the utility of stereotyping, and went to Tilloch and Foulis to obtain practical instructions from them, associating himself also with a London printer, Andrew Wilson. The result was that in 1802 the "plaster" process of stereotyping was perfected. It was the only method in use in the year 1837, and is not altogether abandoned, even up to the present day.

In plaster stereotyping the first operation is that of taking a mould from each page of movable type. Each page is locked up in a separate chase, and it is essential that no particle of dirt or other substance should attach to the bottom of the types so as to prevent them being completely level upon the surface, and that the latter should be perfectly clean and dry. The page is placed upon the lower part of a moulding frame, having previously been rubbed over with an oily composition, and plaster of paris (gypsum) is poured evenly over the whole surface. This sets very quickly, and soon becomes perfectly solid. It is next removed from the surface of the types, in which operation much neatness of hand is required. It requires some dressing with a knife on its edges and is fit for baking —a process which requires a good deal of accurate knowledge. The oven, in which the moulds are placed upon their edges, must be kept at a very regular temperature, for if it be too hot the moulds warp.

The process of casting begins when the moulds have baked sufficiently long to be perfectly dry and hard. The principal utensil is a casting-box at the bottom of which is a movable plate of cast-iron, called a "floating plate." Upon this plate, the face of which is perfectly accurate, the mould is placed with its face downwards. Upon the back of the mould rests the cover of the casting-box, the inside face of whose lid is also perfectly true The cover is held tightly down in the mould by a metal screw. The moulding frame being thus placed in the casting-box, the latter is immersed in an open copper or vessel, holding ten or more hundredweights of metal—chiefly antimony and lead. There are holes in the corners of the cover of the casting-box, through which the liquid metal finds its way into the hollow within. At the instant when the box is plunged into the metal a bubbling noise is heard, which is occasioned by the expulsion of the air contained within the box. After having remained immersed for about ten minutes, it is steadily lifted out by a crane, and swung to a cooling trough, in which the under-side of the box is exposed to water. Being completely cooled, the caster proceeds to remove the mould from the casting-box. The plaster mould, the plate moulded, and the floating plate are all solidly fixed together; and the metal, by its specific gravity, has forced itself under the latter, which it has consequently driven tightly up against the ledges of the mould. The mould has in the same way been driven tightly up against the lid of the casting-box; and the notches in the ledges of the mould have at the same time admitted the metal into the minutest impression from the face of the types. The caster now breaks off the superfluous metal and the ledges of the mould with a wooden mallet. The mould is, of course, destroyed, and if another plate is required another mould must be taken from the types. The plate may now require to be "picked"—that is, if the open spaces of letters have become filled up with little globules of metal, they have to be cleaned or picked out; if any impurities fill up the lines of a wood-cut, these likewise must be removed. The backs of the plates are planed to produce a uniform thickness of metal by a special lathe. They are finally mounted, and made type-high by being fastened to wood, or fixed on metal blocks.

Just previous to the commencement of Her Majesty's reign most of the newspapers made huge strides in regard to circulation, and the mechanical ingenuity of engineers and others was taxed to the utmost to provide greater facilities for producing the largest possible number of copies in the shortest possible time. In 1846 there was introduced into England by an Italian named Vanoni—by trade a maker of plaster casts in statuary—a system of forming moulds in papier-maché. It had been a short time before practised in France. Another Italian, James Dellagana, became acquainted with the system in Paris, and came over here to set up a stereotype foundry. He soon became the most successful stereotyper of his day. In 1855 he patented an invention for casting solid metal plates type high, and also devised a system for casting these plates hollow inside, but still type high, by the use of a core in the casting-box. In 1861 he patented a rolling press for taking the moulds—a great improvement on all previous methods. Between 1856 and 1859 experiments were being made, which led to the most important and permanent results. By 1860 the change from movable type to stereo plates for newspaper printing had been accomplished. The columns were originally cast type high and arranged, after being planed and finished, in a forme of four pages. The next step was to adapt these columns to the rotary Applegath presses. Subsequently, instead of separately dealing with columns, the cast was taken from the complete page at one operation. This was done originally by moulding under the pressure of brushes; afterwards with a roller press. In 1863 the culminating point was reached; plates were cast in a convex form, as required to be fitted on the cylindrical type cylinders of the rotary machines.

BEATING THE STEREOTYPE MATRIX.

In referring to the plaster process, it has been mentioned that only one plate can be cast from one mould. By the paper process a considerable number of casts can be taken from a mould, which is of great importance in newspaper work, as these plates may be placed on several machines and printed from simultaneously. The paper process is also much simpler and more certain than its predecessor. It is much quicker; requires, if done on a small scale, less elaborate apparatus, and is much cheaper. Above all, if the flexible mould is curved, a curved cast may be taken to fit a rotary machine. Attempts were made to cast plates flat and then bend them to make them conform to the shape of the printing cylinder, but without much success.

The stereotyping of bookwork and small commercial compositions by the paper process is a simple and expeditious operation. Type-high clumps are placed round the matter, and the forme is planed and locked up. The face is brushed over with a little oil or is black-leaded, and there is placed on it a "flong," made by pasting together several sheets

CASTING-BOX FOR CURVED PLATES.

of tissue paper to blotting paper, the whole being backed with a sheet of brown paper. The flong is dusted over with French chalk to prevent its adhering to the face of the type. A piece of damp linen is placed over the flong and the operation of beating commenced. A hard brush with a long handle is used for this purpose, which must be brought down upon the forme perfectly flat. In this way the flong is beaten into the type until an impression of the necessary depth is obtained, when a sheet of brown paper is again put over the flong and gently beaten or rolled into it. With a piece of press blanket placed on the top the forme is put into a baking-box and screwed down, and the whole of the moisture evaporated. This converts the flong into a mould, or matrix. This is carefully removed from the forme and examined, and, if perfect, several gauges are placed round the matrix, and a sheet of brown paper placed over them to hang out of the mouth of the casting-box, like the sheet pasted to the matrix. These form a kind of funnel, in which the molten metal is poured upon the face of the matrix, forming the cast. If the

MATRIX AND FINISHED PLATE.

latter is satisfactory, it is trimmed round, and screwed or tacked upon a wooden block, making it the height of type. As already mentioned, many similar casts may be taken from the same mould.

The present system of making plates for rotary machines is much more complicated, and requires special appliances of massive character. Several thicknesses of tissue, blotting, and other stouter papers are used as flong for making the matrix. The flong, when damp and in a pulpy state, is placed over the face of the forme and beaten upon it with a hard, heavy, close-set brush, as shown on the illustration, page 68. After a sufficient beating the type has made a deep impression in the soft pulp. It is then put under a hot press, as shown on the right of the engraving, and left there for a few minutes, until the matrix is dried. It comes off the type quite hard, but flexible. It is then removed into the casting-room, where the molten metal is kept ready for pouring. The flexible matrix, face upwards, is fitted into the hollow part of the casting-box, which is then closed by rolling the cylinder over into the concave part. Between this cylinder and the face of the matrix is about a sixth-of-an-inch, or a pica space. The metal is then poured in, and it runs down and fills all the space between the cylinder and the matrix. After a few seconds the cylinder is rolled out of the hollow part, and on its face is found the curved plate. An illustration (p. 69) shows the casting-box opened after the plate has been cast. The latter is now ready for trimming—that is, for having its ragged edges shaven off by a small circular saw attached to the casting-box. The latest style of casting-box has an improved kind of saw, which renders the use of a separate trimming machine unnecessary. The plate is finally placed in a machine which planes the back so that it may fit the cylinder of the printing machine with perfect accuracy. A single stereo plate for one page of a morning newspaper weighs about 56 lb. The small illustration on the previous page shows the matrix and the finished plate ready for the machine.

The beautiful art of electrotyping, as a method of obtaining fac-simile plates from type or wood-cuts, is distinctly an invention of the Victorian era. It was in 1839 that a paragraph headed "Galvanic Engraving in Relief," in the "Athenæum" announced that "while Mr. Daguerre and Mr. Fox Talbot have been dipping their pencils on the solar spectrum [a reference to the recent discovery of photography] and astonishing us with their inventions, it appears that Prof. Jacobi, at St. Petersburg, has also made a discovery which promises to be of little less importance in the arts. He has found a method—if we understand our informant rightly—of converting any line, however fine, engraved on copper, into a relief by a galvanic process."

The process of electrotyping as carried on in a large establishment involves the use of a good deal of machinery. A moulding case is warmed and placed on a level iron table, and when melted, beeswax is poured into it from a ladle. After the wax has flowed quite level it is rubbed over with black-lead and polished by means of a soft brush, after which it is ready for taking an impression of the block or page to be reproduced. To make this impression, great and steady pressure is needed, and this is obtained from the moulding press—a massive iron frame having a planed bed, over which is a fixed head. There is a projecting table on which the case of wax and the forme of type, which is also black-leaded and brushed, are arranged before sliding them in the press to receive the pressure, which is put on them by raising the bed against the head-piece. After the press is opened, the case and the forme of type are withdrawn and separated. Sometimes a light impression is now taken from the wax. It is next placed on a table for the process of building, which consists in running melted wax on such places of the mould as correspond to blanks in the forme. It is done with the building iron, which is heated and applied to a strip of wax, causing it to melt and flow down on to the blanks. The mould is now ready for black-leading, which is necessary to give it a conducting surface and cause the copper to be gradually deposited over every part of it. The best method is to place the mould on a carriage, which runs forward and backward in an air-tight compartment supplied with black-lead and vibrating brushes which cover the face of the mould thoroughly with the powder, and give it a high polish. The superfluous lead is washed away with water, and by means of another wash, composed of a solution of sulphate of copper and iron-filings, a film of metallic copper is added to the plumbago-covered surface of the

MOULDING AN ELECTROTYPE.

mould. This process, which renders the face of the moulds more conductive after being black-leaded, was discovered about twenty years ago. The magneto-electric machine has, in large establishments, been displaced by the dynamo-electric machine, or dynamo; the distinction being that in the former a permanent magnet is employed, while in the latter its place is taken by an electro-magnet. As the current passes through the bath, the solution becomes decomposed, its copper being gradually deposited on the mould, while the liberated sulphuric acid dissolves an equivalent proportion of copper from the anode; or, in other words, the copper is deposited on the mould at the same rate that it is dissolved from the anode. The first illustration represents an electrotype moulding room, with the dynamo and the battery. On the right, a workman is in the act of raising a mould to ascertain whether the desired thickness of copper shell has been obtained. If this is satisfactory, the mould is taken out of the solu-

FINISHING ELECTROTYPES.

tion, and placed in a slanting position in a trough. Hot water is poured over the back, which melts the surface of the wax in contact with the shell, and the operator removes it from the mould. The shell is then backed with a metal consisting of tin and antimony. The shell is thus thickened to the extent required for use as a plate. It is finally finished by trimming the edges and planing the back. The second illustration shows the electrotype-finishing department of a large establishment.

CHAPTER IX.🍒🍒🍒🍒🍒🍒

PROCESS BLOCKS—LINE BLOCKS—TONE BLOCKS—METHOD OF THEIR PRO-
DUCTION.

THERE are two kinds of process blocks, known as "line blocks" and "tone blocks." The first, of which the "Photo Printing Room" block is a specimen, are made from drawings in pen and ink, and from printed engravings in line and stipple. The drawing is first taken into the photographic studio, in which cameras of unusually large size—some of them capable of producing a negative measuring 24 by 24 inches—are mounted on sliding platforms, as shown in the illustration. In the City of London the electric light is found to be the best illuminant, as the almost invariably murky atmosphere scarcely ever affords sufficient light for the purpose even on the brightest of days. Photographing by electric light can be carried on during the night-time, which is of importance when great despatch in the production of blocks is required. The plate glass for the negative is prepared in the customary manner of the collodion process, and after exposure in the camera the plate goes to the dark room, where it is developed. It is afterwards intensified and fixed. After this it goes to the printing room, the arrangements of which may be as shown in the illustration. This stage of the process is one of the most important features of the art of photo-etching, as much of the ultimate success depends upon the proper preparation of the zinc plate upon which the picture is transferred from the negative. All blemishes, such as spots and scratches, have to be carefully obliterated, and the surface must be highly polished, without having an extreme smoothness. For this reason the plate is immersed in a weak acid bath, which gives it a grained character. A sensitising solution is then poured over the plate, which is next dried over gas. It is next placed on the negative in a printing frame in the manner adopted by photographers generally. The negative is placed on the glass, and the sensitised zinc pressed firmly and evenly upon it by boards and screws. The glazed front is exposed to the powerful rays of the electric light for a period regulated by the power of the

PHOTOGRAPHIC STUDIO FOR REPRODUCTION FOR PROCESS BLOCKS.

illuminant and the density wished for in the negative. This is ascertained by the use of the actinometer. When sufficiently exposed the plate is removed from the frame, rolled up with lithographic transfer ink, and developed in a bath containing water. By gently rubbing with cotton wool the sensitised film is removed, except in those places where the light has acted upon it through the picture. The parts so fixed are the actual lines of the original picture, which now appears black on a light ground.

The plate is dried, the entire surface covered with gum arabic, dried again, and again rolled up with ink. All this gives the lines of the drawing a firm acid "resist," the ink being fixed to the plate by means of a coating of resin. What is called "retouching" may, however, be necessary at this stage in order to rectify the defects of the original from which the photograph was taken. When dry, the plate is taken to a litho press, and an impression on transfer paper from a copper-plate having the required tint engraved upon it is placed upon the zinc plate, and the whole run

PHOTO PRINTING-ROOM FOR PROCESS WORK.

through the litho press. It will then be found that, except where the surface has been gummed, the lines or dots have been transferred to the spaces originally assigned to them by the artist. The plate next goes to the etching-room, of which an illustration is appended. Here the large surfaces which will appear white when printed, are painted out by a solution of shellac, which resists acid, and when this is dry the plate is given a first bath of very much diluted nitric acid. This mixture is contained in a very large earthenware pan or trough. One effect of the action of the acid upon the metal is the formation of oxides and air bubbles, which have to be got rid of, either by gently swaying the trough, which is balanced on rockers, so as to keep the acid in motion, or by a system of brushing the plates while in the bath with a camel-hair brush. Every plate must go through various stages of etching in baths of various strengths, but between each bath the more delicate parts of the design are painted out, and the plate rolled up. At length there remain only the large spaces, which must be eaten away to a considerable depth by the nitric acid. The plate is cleaned, and a proof is pulled on the press in order to judge the

ETCHING-ROOM FOR PROCESS WORK.

result. If defects are observable they may be rectified by an engraver. The plate is finally mounted on a wood block, generally of oak, to make it type-high.

For reproducing photographs, drawings in wash, pencil, and chalk, and all kinds of paintings and drawings in colour, the "half-tone" process is employed. The expression "half-tone" is a translation into English of the familiar art phrase, "mezzo-tinto." The distinctive feature of a process block of this kind is that the various tones in the original are reproduced, not by lines, but by minute dots. The illustration, "Photographic Studio," is an example of this style of process block. The dots are not always detected by the unassisted eye, but they can be readily perceived by the use of a magnifying glass. This texture is produced by means of a screen placed in the camera between the lens and the negative. The screen may be formed by two sheets of glass attached to each other, each having upon its inner surface a series of minutely-engraved parallel lines. On one plate these lines are vertical, and on the other horizontal, or they may be engraved diagonally, to the right and left respectively. The engraved lines cut up into minute squares the image of the picture as it appears in the negative. The subsequent processes for making the tone block are substantially the same as for the line block. In order to "bite in" the plate it is passed through weak acid and rolled up with ink. It is then laid in a stone trough containing an acid solution to be "deep etched"—that is, until the acid has eaten away all that is necessary of the darkest portion of the picture. Every plate goes through several baths, between each of which it is dusted with an acid-resisting powder, and proofs are taken during the progress of the work.

The introduction of the half-tone block has almost revolutionised modern methods of printing. The old conditions of using damp paper and a blanketed cylinder have had to be abandoned, and a special paper produced to suit the new kind of illustration. A wood-cut is almost as easily printed as a type forme, on account of the high relief of the surface, but the tone process block is so slightly in relief that its depth is not appreciable to the touch. To obtain a fine impression super-calendered paper has to be used, in which all the microscopic interstices have been levelled up by filling them with a calcareous deposit, and finishing by heavy rolling. The printing machine has had to be re-modelled by making it three times as strong to bear the strain of the rigidity of the cylinder when in contact with the hard copper blocks.

CHAPTER X.🌰🌰🌰🌰🌰🌰

INK MANUFACTURE—IMPORTANCE OF THE COMMODITY—SCIENTIFIC SKILL
INVOLVED—MODERN MATERIALS AND PROCESSES.

INCE the days when Johnson, as mentioned in a previous page, had so much difficulty in obtaining a black ink, with which an ordinary wood-cut could be satisfactorily printed, great strides have been made in the manufacture of what has been called the greatest civiliser that the world has ever known—the lubricator which keeps the intellectual machinery of the world in motion through the impressions it makes. In Johnson's time there were makers of inks for printers, but they contented themselves with a wooden shanty, or outbuilding, under the roof of which—in some cases the shanty did not possess a roof at all, for it was thought more economical in so dangerous a business to be prepared for a "flare-up" by having no roof to catch alight than to pay insurance money—was the furnace built in one corner, suspended above which was the oil-boiler. The varnish-maker and his boy would have to superintend the whole of the operations of boiling the oil into varnish, ready to be incorporated into the pigment. The method followed was the time-honoured one of rule-o'-thumb, and the capacity of the maker for overcoming any unexpected difficulties was limited by his experience. On the skill of this man depended the successful issue of a perfect product. In this rough-and-ready way was the varnish prepared; in a similar inconvenient and rough way was the ink itself compounded by men who ground up the pigment and vehicle on a stone or marble slab by the aid of a muller. The labour was tedious and slow; but pounds of ink only were made and used then, where tons are used now.

In the entire range of the industrial arts there are few manufactured products which demand more skill in the technical operations than modern ink-making, or one in which such extraordinary care is rendered necessary if satisfactory results are to be attained. Each of the manufacturing operations peculiar to ink-making partakes of a scientific character to a marked degree.

A modern ink factory comprises many separate departments. In one there will be a series of receiving tanks and a row of vessels used in the production of phthallic acid—a compound of carbon, hydrogen, and oxygen, used chiefly in the making of aniline colours. It is obtained from naphthaline, which, on being attacked by nitric acid yields this acid, and a series of nitro-substitution products. There will be probably appliances for making nitric acid. Saltpetre (nitrate of potash), and sulphuric acid are placed in suitable retorts, when by an interchange of components between the two bodies the solid potash salt is converted into the nitric acid, while the sulphuric acid has become converted into a sulphate of potash. During this transposition between the components used the nitric acid first rises as a gas, which becomes condensed and flows into stoneware receivers as a liquid. There will also be provided in the factory means for the recovery of oil and spirits which would otherwise be wasted.

In preparing and grinding the colour ready for mixing with the printers' varnish or other vehicle, great care and attention to cleanliness are required, for any dust, grit, or other impurity in the colour would spoil the product. By means of ponderous edge-runners, or vertical millstones, the colour after mixing with the vehicle is reduced to a paste, ready to be finally ground and incorporated by granite roller mills. Pigmenting colours are obtained in various ways. Some are solids precipitated from solutions of the various chemical salts; others are produced by cooking the ingredients, while others are obtained from natural sources, as earths, etc. Whatever the source of origin, the solid colour has to be washed, dried, and ground, if in lumps, before it is fit to mix with a vehicle into an ink or paint. All these operations are tedious, and demand

Caxton Window, Stationers' Hall.

time and labour. The first of the accompanying illustrations shows a colour-grinding room; in the second illustration is depicted the operation of mixing the dry colour with the printers' varnish. Along one side of the room may be noticed a row of granite roller mills. The ink, having previously been mixed to a paste with the vehicle, is put on the rollers of these machines, and as they revolve the colour is intimately mixed and incorporated with the vehicle. Each machine requires constant attention,

COLOUR GRINDING ROOM.

for the colour, as it spreads out on the rollers, has to be scraped off the rollers and replaced in the centre, and, moreover, each colour requires a definite amount of grinding. Since some colours require much longer grinding than others before they become incorporated with the vehicle, the edge-runner mill is first used for mixing the dry powder with the paste by incorporating it with oil or varnish; but this paste is not at all fine enough to be used as printers' ink, and so the paste has to be further ground by the roller mills shown in the picture. Some pigments are in lumps, such as Prussian blue, indigo, etc., and these lumps have first to be crushed before mixing to a paste, and the crushing mill is shown in the corner of the illustration. The pigment to be crushed is put into the copper, whence it falls into the interior of the machine, wherein are

suitable revolving surfaces which pulverise the lumps as they pass through
To make a factory of any pretensions thoroughly complete, it is absolutely
necessary to provide a chemical laboratory, where the chemist and his
assistants can carry out their investigations of the products of the firm
before passing them on for sale, and also for analysing and testing the
purity and quality of the raw material used by the firm.

During the past sixty years the quality of the printing inks produced
has been improved to the extent of 50 or 75 per cent., while the prices

INK FACTORY.

at which they have been sold have decreased in the same proportion. A
news ink which cost a shilling a pound at the beginning of the reign can
now be had for fourpence.

The printing inks which were purchaseable even thirty years ago were
either black, or colours prepared from mineral substances. There was dull
red obtained from ochres and oxides of iron, and the more brilliant
although less stable vermilion, a compound of mercury and sulphur. Car-
mine, however, prepared by precipitating the colouring matter obtained
from an insect by means of alumina and ammonia, was used to a certain

extent to brighten dull reds, and resist the bleaching action of light. There was blue in a variety of forms, such as ultramarine, which used to be obtained from the rare mineral lapsis lazuli, but is now prepared by heating white clay with salts of iron and soda; Prussian blue and smaltz. There was a variety of shades of green and yellow, with a few browns, and these were nearly all that were at the disposal of printers. Since then an entirely new class of colours have sprung into existence—colours obtained from coal tar. From this filthy, foul-smelling body, chemical skill has arrested, or almost created, a vast array of beautiful and useful products, some of which exceed in brilliancy almost the flowers with which they vie. In addition to these, so-called "art shades"—blue, green, olive, and deep reds, subdued or saddened with a small percentage of black— have come into favour with printers, especially since some of the illus- trated newspapers issued supplements of reproductions of Royal Academy and other pictures printed in these subdued colours. The effect, if the shades are judiciously selected, is very pleasing; but if not, is very ridiculous, as a print of a seascape in bright geranium-red, a moonlight effect in salmon- pink, and an ancestral banqueting hall in violet. Plain black ink on white or slightly tinted paper is decidedly preferable to any other for the text of a book, but there is no reason why it should predominate every- where. We have quite sufficient and to spare of it in our modern cloth- ing, whilst in nature, which is the best guide in matters appertaining to colouring, we find very little black indeed.

CHAPTER XI. 🌸🌸🌸🌸🌸🌸🌸

PAPER MANUFACTURE—MATERIALS—METHODS IN USE AT A MODERN MILL.

THE only materials employed for the manufacture of paper in former times were linen and cotton rags, flax and hemp waste, and a few other fibre-yielding materials. In the first year of Her Majesty's reign the excise duty on paper of 3d. per pound was reduced to 1½d. This caused an immensely increased demand for paper. Manufacturers exhibited much anxiety lest the supply of rags should prove insufficient for their needs. The excise duty was totally abolished in 1861. Immediately a great number of journals were brought out in all parts of the Kingdom, and cheap reprints of standard authors made their appearance and were sold in vast quantities. This produced an enormously increased demand for paper. Had other materials than those employed before the repeal of the duty not been discovered, the abolition of the impost would have proved of limited service to the public at large. The ingenuity of man, however, averted the inconvenience which would have arisen, and entirely new materials were experimented on and adopted for the manufacture of cheap paper. Some of these are now of the highest importance in the paper trade, and the quantity of rag paper now made bears a very small proportion indeed to that made of other material.

The materials now used are, besides rags, esparto grass, wood, straw, and waste paper. Linen and cotton rags are imported into Great Britain from nearly all the countries of Europe, and even from South America,

Africa, and Australia. A large proportion comes from Germany. Esparto is a fibrous grass obtained in the South of Spain and in North Africa. Immense quantities of wood, in the form of pulp, come from Norway, Sweden, and Germany, and by many it is thought that wood as an inexhaustible source of useful fibre, will probably be the principal material employed. The extraction of the fibre of wood is obtained by chemical processes, such as boiling it, when chipped, in caustic soda, or treating it in sulphuric acid; or by mechanical processes, such as by pressing blocks of wood against a revolving grindstone, which reduces the material to a more or less fine condition, but not in a powdery form.

No manufacturer did so much to develop the paper trade and to utilise these newly-discovered materials as the late Mr. Edward Lloyd. In the year 1861 the weekly consumption of paper in his own establishment had reached so large a quantity that he found it necessary to start a paper mill to supply his own requirements. Owing to the falling-off, a little time after, of the supply of rags, some other raw material had to be substituted. Attention was turned to the newly-discovered esparto grass, and properties in Algeria and the South of

MR. EDWARD LLOYD.

Spain were purchased, along with the rights to collect the produce over large tracts of land. In 1877 Mr. Lloyd found it necessary to erect another mill, at Sittingbourne. Shortly after, the manufacture of wood pulps was undertaken. A large property was purchased at Honefos, in Norway, having an available water force of 12,000 horse power. The mills are surrounded on all sides by enormous forests, from which the trees are cut to make the pulp. They are then thrown into the river, to float down unassisted to the mills, at no cost whatever. When the process of converting the timber into pulp has been completed, the prepared material is sent down to the port and put on board the firm's steamers. It may not be uninteresting to say that the carriage of pulp from Norway to Sittingbourne is actually less than the cost of carting it from one extremity of London to the other.

Although it is impossible within the space at our disposal to give a connected account of the many processes involved in the manufacture of a sheet of paper, a brief outline may be sketched, first of the old method of hand-making—not, yet, by any means, discarded—and then the modern method of machine-making of rag and straw papers.

The two most important changes that have taken place in the manufacture of paper during the last sixty years are those resulting from the use of two materials, used as a substitute for rags—esparto grass and wood pulp. Practically, the pioneer in both these developments was the late Mr. Edward Lloyd.

PAPER-MAKING BY HAND.

For the purpose of making paper by hand the appliances were few and simple, consisting of a vat, to contain the pulp, with a steam pipe or other appliance for keeping up the heat, and an agitator to prevent the matter settling. There was also required the mould—a frame of wood, with parallel or crossed wires running across it. These wires left their impression on the soft pulp, producing the "water-marked" lines of a laid hand-made paper. The vatman, standing at the vat, took in his hand the mould and a wooden frame, which, when laid upon the mould, formed with it a shallow tray of wire. This was called the "deckle." He dipped the mould and the deckle into the vat, and took up sufficient pulp to form a sheet of paper of the weight he was engaged upon, and he poured back what was superfluous. This was a very delicate and clever operation, for he had nothing to guide him as to the thickness of the paper, except his own sense of feeling. His experience and practice, however, enabled him to make sheet after sheet with a variation of not more than a grain or two between them. He shook the mould first from his breast outwards and back again, then from right to left, and back again. By these movements the pulp was propelled in four directions, and it was thereby caused to interweave itself or to "felt," the water meanwhile escaping through the wire. The mould and the new formed sheet were next passed on to a board, and the deckle removed. An assistant, called the coucher, removed the mould and sheet, and turned it upside down on a piece of felt, to which the paper was transferred. When about half-a-dozen quires of paper were thus made, with felts between each sheet, the pile was taken to a press and compressed. A boy, called a layer, separated the sheets and the flannels. The latter were returned to the coucher, and the sheets went under the press again, remaining there all night, with the view of getting rid of more of the moisture. On the following day the paper was again separated and pressed. The quantity made by two men and a boy in a day was about six or eight reams. The sheets were next dried over hair ropes in a room which used to be known as the "loft"; hence the term "loft-dried papers." Sizing the sheets came next. They were passed through a long trough containing a solution of gelatine, which "sized" the paper. Before this sizing it was as absorbent as blotting paper. The sheets were again dried and glazed and sorted, the "perfect" sheets being counted into reams.

CUTTING THE RAGS.

We now turn to the methods in use in a modern mill, beginning with the treatment of the rags. When the bales arrive at the mill, they are sorted, and cut into small pieces. Care is taken to remove from them any buttons, tapes, hooks or eyes, or any other adjuncts which fitted them for the clothing of human beings. This work is done by women, and each worker has in front of her a table, and receptacles into which she can sort her rags as fast as she can cut them into pieces. The cutting is done by putting the rags across an oblique knife—generally formed from part of a scythe—which projects from the surface of each table or work bench. The rags are next placed in a large boiler, where they are boiled and bleached in solution of lime and soda ash. The boiling and bleaching are continued in the rag-washing engine, where a continuous stream of water carries off the dirt, while knives tear the rags into a fine pulp. Soaking for some hours in a bleaching solution follows next, and, after

RAG-WASHING ENGINE HOUSE, SITTINGBOURNE MILLS.

a further washing in water, the pulp is again cut up and reduced in a machine called the beater. In this engine, which will be referred to in dealing with straw papers, the pulp is prepared for being made into paper by the hand or machine process by the addition of other qualities of pulp, of clay, etc., to form paper of the kind or quality required. Here, too, the size—which is a soap, composed of resin and alum—is added, and the colouring matter, if required, is also added, the whole being thoroughly mixed.

The treatment of esparto is necessarily very considerably different. The bales of grass, when opened, are shaken and dusted, to get rid of sand and other substances. The grass is placed in a large iron cylinder, where it is whirled swiftly round by a toothed drum. The dust is sucked downwards by a powerful fan through an opening in the bottom of the cylinder, and the grass is automatically passed out and up an inclined plane.

DUSTING ESPARTO GRASS.

The grass is then put into boilers, along with a solution of caustic soda, at a pressure of 10 to 40 lb. to the square inch. It is here boiled until quite soft, and all dust is loosened. The illustration represents the

RAKING OUT A CYLINDER.

process of raking out a cylinder, after the esparto grass has been boiled in it. The boiled grass is next put in boxes or barrows, and taken to the "breaker." The breaker, or washer, is an enormous vat, or engine, of a peculiar shape. The mass of softened rags or grass is kept in a continual rapid movement. It passes a revolving cylinder, or paddle-wheel beater, armed with sharp knives, by which the small pieces are gradually cut up and beaten into a thick pulp. The constant stream of water, entering by a pump, goes through the mass, and the revolving sieve, called a drum-washer, allows the water and dirt to escape by a waste pipe.

From the breakers the pulp flows into a lower set of engines called the "potchers." Hitherto the pulp is of the natural colour of the grass, but in the potchers it is bleached by a mixture of chloride of lime or chlorine. Girls, standing around the edges of the engine, fish out with broad flat wooden spoons the small bits of root or knots of grass which

A BREAKER.

otherwise would show as specks in the paper. When the bleaching agent is washed out nothing remains but fibre and water.

The pulp is next taken to the beating house. It is now so fine and

PULP FLOWING INTO MACHINE.

white that a little of it placed in a bowl of clean water dissolves, and when the bowl is shaken the water assumes the appearance of milk. It would require a microscope to distinguish the minute atoms into which the grass or rags have been reduced. The beating is of the nature of a powerful churning, and its object is to free the pulp of the chlorine, which otherwise would give the paper when dry a yellowish tinge. It has a yet further object. The natural colour of the paper, freed from the chlorine, would be a light-green neutral shade instead of white. To produce this a very little ultramarine blue and cochineal is put into the pulp and is thoroughly churned up with it in the beating engine.

PAPER-MAKING MACHINE.

The pulp is now led by a pipe to the stuff "chest"—an enormous circular vat, some 9 feet deep by 12 in diameter. This is simply the reservoir in which the pulp is stored till wanted. The pulp is kept at the proper consistency by a continual agitation. It is now ready for the machine, which is to convert it into paper. As the pulp is needed, it is pumped up into a smaller chest, elevated over the head of the machine. The latter is a complicated arrangement of small rollers and cylinders of various sizes, extending nearly the whole length of a long room.

The small illustration on the previous page shows the head of the paper-making machine, into which the pulp is poured in a thin watery stream. By

REELING MACHINE, SITTINGBOURNE MILLS.

the turning of a handle the flow of the pulp can be so regulated as to determine at will the weight or thickness of the paper.

In the machine, the pulp, after flowing down on to sand "tables," passes through strainers that purify it from any infinitesimal atoms of hard substances that may have escaped it thus far. It flows on to a float frame, or cloth, of very fine brass wire that is moving continually forward on rollers. This endless wire has a shaking motion, and allows the water to escape, while retaining the fibre evenly spread out. The wire, carrying with it the residuum of pulp, passes under the dandy roll—a cylinder coated with fine wire that presses on the pulp and gives it the watermark. It is now paper, although in a limp, damp, and almost pulpy condition.

The paper is next passed between a pair of couching rolls, which press it still further, and it issues forth for the first time a self-supporting endless sheet. It next goes between press rolls, and gets the water still further

PAPER MACHINE-ROOM, SITTINGBOURNE MILLS.

pressed out. After this it goes over and under a series of cylinders, heated by steam, which rapidly dry it. Then it travels between two intermediate rolls, and then over a second set of drying cylinders. It now goes through the calender—a series of chilled iron rolls that give it a surface. From the last of these rolls it is wound up in the form of a reel, which may be four miles in length. The illustration shows the continuous sheet passing over the last set of drying cylinders and the calender, and being reeled off. It is now ready for being sent to the printing office, if it is to be printed in the web.

For papers that are of a higher quality and are not to be printed in the reel, further treatment is necessary. If extra finish is required, the reels are taken to the super-calender, where both sides are glazed by great pressure and heat. The reels are then cut into sheets. These are taken to the finishing house, where each sheet is examined, and faulty ones are thrown out. The sheets are then counted into quires and reams, and packed.

The largest output of any mill in the world is that of Messrs Edward Lloyd and Sons' mill at Sittingbourne, five miles distant from the mouth of the Thames. It was started in 1877, the weekly production beginning at 50 tons, and increasing year by year, until the quantity made weekly amounts to nearly 600 tons. The illustration gives an idea of a portion of one of the paper machine rooms. The machines turn out paper from 100 to 126 inches wide. To give the reader some idea of the quantity produced, it may be mentioned that about 600,000 miles of paper, one yard in width, are made annually—long enough to reach the moon and leave a good deal of margin after returning to mother earth, or, if reduced to a one-inch strip, the sun, a distance of 95,000,000 miles, could be reached with less than five years' output. The annual product, reduced to a yard in width, would go more than twenty times round the circumference of this planet.

CHAPTER XII. ❦❦❦❦❦❦

HIS memento of the Queen's Diamond Jubilee has been produced almost entirely by letterpress methods which are distinctly inventions of the Victorian era.

If a book of this kind had to be printed sixty years ago, its illustrations must have been wood engravings, and the text matter must have been set up in movable types.

It has now become possible to dispense with both cuts and types. The blocks are exclusively "process" blocks ; the reading matter has been composed in Linotype bars. Hence the book is a specimen of typography executed without the use of types, and of engraving without the use of the graver.

The reader will be able to judge for himself whether, from an artistic point of view, the work has in any way suffered from being produced by the new methods. It may be added that on the grounds of rapidity and economy of production they have an enormous advantage over the processes they have to a large extent superseded. The Linotype bars were set up at a speed five or six times quicker than the matter could have been composed in movable type, and with a saving of 40 to 50 per cent. in cost. The blocks were each made in three or four hours, and on an average for one-fifth to one-tenth of the price that would have been charged for wood engravings. To this extent, at least, the book is in itself an exemplification of the progress made in printing during the reign of Queen Victoria.

The compiler is indebted to several gentlemen for their courteous permission to reproduce illustrations which have appeared in their publications. Special acknowledgements are due to

Sir GEO. NEWNES, for Example of Art Poster for the " Weekly Dispatch."

Messrs. JAMES CLARKE & CO., 13 & 14, Fleet Street, E.C., for illustrations from their booklet, "How the 'Christian World' is Produced"—viz., Delivery of Paper in Reels, Reel Damping Machine, Hoe Supplement Press, Delivery at Machine, Beating Stereo Matrix, Casting-Box for Curved Plates, Matrix and Finished Plate, Cutting Rags, Dusting Grass, Raking Out Cylinder, Breaker, Pulp in Machine, and Paper-Making Machine.

Mr. HORACE HART, M.A., Controller, University Press, Oxford, for the Portrait, from his Memoir, of Earl Stanhope.

Mr. HERBERT LLOYD (Messrs. Edward Lloyd & Son, Salisbury Square, proprietors of the Sittingbourne Paper Mills), for View of a Reeling Machine and Paper Machine Room.

Messrs. MACKELLAR, SMITHS, & JORDAN, Philadelphia, U.S.A., for view of Room in a Modern Type-Foundry; and the Processes of Moulding an Electrotype and Finishing Electrotypes, taken from "One Hundred Years," a History of their Type-Foundry.

Messrs. JOHN SWAIN & SON, 58, Farringdon Street, E.C., for views of a Process Block Photographic Studio, Photo Printing Room, and Etching Room.

EDITOR, "British & Colonial Printer & Stationer," for view of a Colour-Grinding Room, an Ink Factory, and Paper-Making by Hand.

With the exception of the blocks by Mr. Sedgwick and Messrs. John Swain & Son, the whole of the process work was done by Messrs. Hare and Co., Ltd., Bride Court, E.C. The head-pieces to the chapters, the initial letters, and the tail-pieces are from the collection of typographical embellishments belonging to Mr. Geo. W Jones, St. Bride House, Dean Street, Fetter Lane, E.C., on whose presses the entire book has been printed.

THE ROYAL PORTRAITS.

The frontispiece, "Her Majesty Queen Victoria in Coronation Robes," is from a painting in the Royal Collection, by Sir G. Hayter, R.A., reproduced in "Sixty Years a Queen," by Sir Herbert Maxwell, Bart., M.P. Messrs. Harmsworth Bros., Ltd., publishers of the work, and Messrs. Eyre and Spottiswoode, the Queen's printers, kindly permitted the copying of this engraving.

The other portrait, "Her Majesty Queen Victoria in 1897," is from a photograph taken by the firm of W. & D. Downey, Ebury Street, S.W. This is a fine example of Half-Tone Process work by Mr. W F. Sedgwick, Ltd., photo-etcher, artist, and designer, 236 and 237, Blackfriars Road, S.E.

THE CAXTON WINDOW, ST. MARGARET'S, WESTMINSTER.

The design of this window, which was unveiled in 1882, was prepared by Mr. Henry Holiday. In the central division is a picture representing Caxton standing in front of his press, and holding a printed book in his hand. On a scroll are the titles of some of his principal works. The artist, aware that the familiar portrait of Caxton was known to be spurious, has designed an ideal figure. Above is the well-known mark, and the sign of the red pale; while elsewhere are the words "Fiat Lux," and the date 1477, the year when Caxton is supposed to have set up his press at Westminster. In the centre of the tracery are the Arms of Kent, where Caxton was born, and in the panels at the base of the window are the Arms of London, where he made his position in life, of Bruges, where he learnt the art of printing, and of Westminster, where he practised it in England. A part of the canopy work is occupied by figures, representing Religion, Art, Science, and Philosophy. On each side of the figure of Caxton are depicted two well-known men, who might be taken as representatives of the Old and New Learning. On the left hand is a picture of the Venerable Bede, habited as a monk, and in the right hand light is Erasmus, one of the great promoters of the New Learning to which printing may be said to have given birth.

THE CAXTON WINDOW, STATIONERS' HALL.

This window, by Mayer & Co., Munich, was unveiled in July, 1894. The central idea represents Caxton submitting a proof to King Edward IV and his Queen, in the Almonry of Westminster Abbey. Beside the King stands a figure of Edward V. In the left foreground is seated a boy busily grinding materials for the ink, and directly behind him is the press. In the left background a compositor is engaged arranging the types. In the centre appears the arms of the Stationers' Company, with the date of the Company's Charter (1556), supported by angels on either side holding the Mitre and Pastoral Cross of the Archbishop of Canterbury, the patron of the Company. At the foot is represented the ancient barge of the Company floating upon the Thames. The domed border is fitted with medallions containing the devices of eminent printers—viz., William Seres, Reginald Wolf, Wynkyn de Worde, Richard Tottel, Richard Jugge, John Day, John Cawood, and Hugh Singleton.

Her Majesty Queen Victoria in 1897.